PRAISE AND APPRECIATION FOR
LIFE *Worth* LIVING
AND THE EDEN ALTERNATIVE

"This book offers a splendid solution for those who feel that death might be the best alternative to old age. A provocative, inspiring, hopeful work."—BOOKLIST

"Excellent book . . . worth reading for anyone involved in selecting any type of living facility for an older relative or friend."—SOUTHERN LIFESTYLES

"This book is an inspiring account of Edenizing [the Chase Memorial Nursing Home], emphasizing the benefits to residents and staff."—LIBRARY JOURNAL

"One nursing home resident, formerly so depressed that she remained silent, now wanders down hallways chirping a duet with a songbird on her shoulder. . . . Some locations maintain barns and gardens or share space with kindergartens and summer camps."—U.S. NEWS & WORLD REPORT

"This book is a gold mine of resources, ideas, addresses, and what to do and not do. As we age, wouldn't we all want to be in a community that is committed to truly caring? Truly [Dr. Thomas's] vision is of a place of *life*!"—CRONE CHRONICLES

"Although this book is primarily about improving the nursing home setting with the Eden Alternative, these improvements are adaptable to the family home setting as well. . . . It is an exceptional read."—CAREGIVER MONTHLY

"The Revolution has begun. . . . Thousands of our elders will live longer, happier, more fulfilling lives because of this most gentle and insightful of people."—DANNY SIEGEL, LECTURER AND AUTHOR

"*Life Worth Living* is essential reading for anyone with a family member or friend in nursing care, for anyone charged with the nursing home care of residents, for social workers, health care workers, and senior citizen centers' reference shelves."—THE MIDWEST BOOK REVIEW

"For those dealing with institutionalization, Thomas provides hope that this does not have to be the experience dreaded by many."—PUBLISHERS WEEKLY

"The book explains the Eden philosophy and provides a blueprint for putting it into action, from reorganization of staff into teams right down to recommended type of cat litter. [Said one administrator:] 'I wouldn't go back. We were good before, but we're so much better now.' [Another said:] 'It has become a place to live instead of a place to die'."—ASSOCIATED PRESS

AWARDS

A BOOK OF THE YEAR IN GERONTOLOGICAL NURSING
American Journal of Nursing

HONORABLE MENTION — MEDICAL BOOK AWARDS
American Medical Writers Association

1997 AMERICA'S AWARD
"Like a Nobel Prize in Goodness" given to
William H. Thomas, M.D.

LIFE *Worth* LIVING

How Someone You Love Can Still Enjoy Life in a Nursing Home

The Eden Alternative in Action

William H. Thomas, M.D.

VanderWyk & Burnham
Acton, Massachusetts

Published by VanderWyk & Burnham
A Division of Publicom, Inc.
Acton, Massachusetts

This publication is sold with the understanding that the publisher is not engaged in rendering legal, medical, or other professional services. If expert assistance is required, the services of a competent professional person should be sought.

Acknowledgment is gratefully given for permission to include these works of others: Judy Meyers Thomas for the photographs that appear on the center-insert pages with figures 2, 3, 4, and 8; Herb Ryan for the photograph that appears on the center-insert page with figure 5; and David Betler for the photograph that appears on the center-insert page with figure 6.

Publisher's Cataloging-in-Publication Data
Thomas, William H., M.D.
Life Worth Living: How Someone You Love Can Still Enjoy Life in a
    Nursing Home—The Eden Alternative in Action / William H.
    Thomas, M.D.
1. Nursing home care. 2. Institutional care—Psychological aspects.
I. Title.
RA997.T69   362.16   96-60382
ISBN: 0-9641089-6-8

Portions of this book were previously published as *The Eden Alternative: Nature, Hope & Nursing Homes.*

Manufactured in the United States of America
10 9 8 7 6 5 4 3

*Dedicated to my wife Judy
and a marriage made in Eden*

✧   ✧   ✧

This is the bitterest pain among men,
to have much knowledge but no power.

—*Herodotus*

A passionate interest in what you do
is the secret of enjoying life,
perhaps the secret of long life,
whether it is helping old people or children
or making cheese or growing earthworms.

—*Julia Child*

One thing is certain,
and I have always known it—
the joys of my life have nothing to do with age.

—*May Sarton*

Contents

Preface   xi

Introduction   1

Part 1: Taking Care ——————————

  1   The Truth about Nursing Homes   7

  2   The Confusion of Care, Treatment, and Kindness   17

  3   Nature, Hope, and Nursing Homes   27

  4   The First Eden Alternative   35

  5   Medication Reduction   47

  6   Death in the Nursing Home   55

  7   The Administrator as Leader   61

  8   Empowering Employees   71

Part 2: Building Human Habitats ——————————

  9   The Vision   89

  10   Children   99

  11   Dogs   111

  12   Cats   121

  13   Birds   127

  14   Other Animals   139

  15   Plants   143

  16   The Garden   155

  17   The Risks   163

  18   Other Places   171

Afterword   175

Epilogue   181

    Pet Resources 183
    Foliage Plants Recommended for Nursing Homes 186
    Garden Supplies 189
    Indoor and Outdoor Gardening Bibliography 191
    Acknowledgments 199
    Index 201

Preface

In four years at Harvard Medical School,
I never set foot inside a nursing home.

Believe me when I tell you, I never expected to wind up working in a nursing home. Like most doctors, my passion for professional success left me with no desire to see the words "nursing home doctor" attached to my name. I had better places to be and more important things to do. I went out of my way to avoid nursing homes.

That was then. Today, I am proud of my nursing home practice and my patients. I find that caring for nursing home residents is a task of limitless challenge and variety. My patients have taught me what scores of professors could not. Patients understand the enormous difference between simply receiving treatment and being well cared for. They have helped me come to terms with both the art and the science of medicine.

Earlier in my career, science had the upper hand. I was admitted to Harvard Medical School in the spring of 1982. My four years in Boston were a blessing to me. My teachers and the hospitals in which they worked were among the best in the world. There was, of course, a price to pay for this excellence, and it went beyond the cost of tuition. As medical students, we were immersed in a world where the highest degree of respect was earned by diagnosing rare and interesting diseases. We understood that the ability to prattle on about patients with unusual medical conditions was an important element of success. Patients afflicted with the ordinary burdens of age, disability, and decay, on the other hand, were of much less interest to the medical staff and their students. With the often cutting humor of the medical profession, the elderly, and particularly the frail, demented elderly, were referred to by nasty, demeaning names that do not bear repeating. In four years at Harvard Medical School, I never set foot inside a nursing home.

After graduation, I decided against specializing and signed on for the family medicine program at the University of Rochester. These family doctors worked from distinctly non-Harvard assumptions; they cultivated a holistic view that encompassed patients, their families, and communities. Time with these doctors was well spent, but as interns and residents, we logged many more hours in the hospitals, working with specialists.

As a resident physician, I found great pleasure in my rotations on the obstetric and pediatric services. Working with children and expectant mothers allowed me to share in the vitality and vigor of early life. Babies I delivered as an intern were toddling about and calling my name by the end of my final year of training. I learned that it was my job to clear away as many obstacles as possible for these kids so they could grow and develop.

While I took pleasure from my time spent in labor and delivery rotations, making rounds in the nursing home was like a dose of castor oil: necessary, perhaps, but extremely unpleasant. In the nursing home, I felt like a shipbuilder who had been mistakenly assigned to the salvage yard. My patients got sicker, weaker, and more withdrawn as time passed, and when one died, he or she was promptly replaced with another who was cruising down life's off-ramp. After finishing my residency, I was free to fulfill my personal pledge never to set foot into another nursing home. Or so I thought.

I joined a small-town family practice and took the place of the group's departing senior partner. I was pleased to find that he had a booming obstetric practice, which I was happy to assume. I was also informed that he had a busy nursing home practice, and about that I was not as happy. Like most private practitioners, I squeezed my visits to the nursing home in between trips to the hospital and the grocery store. I was often annoyed by the frequent phone calls and the paperwork hassles. I felt that my efforts were in vain. After all, how could I take care of people who were so far gone? What good could I really do for them?

For this and other reasons, private practice lost its appeal, and I began to look for different work. When I was offered a position as an emergency room physician in a thirty-bed rural hospital, I took it and left.

As an emergency room doctor, I diagnosed heart attacks, delivered babies, casted fractures, and counseled the suicidal. I became the ultimate Mr. Fix-It. The variety and challenge excited me, but the hours took their toll, and I missed building relationships with my patients. After a couple of years, I was ready for a change. One warm spring afternoon, my phone rang. The administrator of a nearby nursing home was on the line. Would I consider becoming the medical director and only physician for their eighty-bed nursing home? I said no. He called back two days later.

"How about if you just come down for a look?"

I said, "Maybe."

He called again and asked whether Friday would be a good day for me to visit.

I said, "Okay."

Three weeks later, still wondering what I had gotten myself into, I was a nursing home doctor.

❖   ❖   ❖

My new job required that I rethink my prejudices and biases about nursing homes. On the one hand, I found the possibility of a nurturing, supportive home for the frail, ill elderly to be a warm and civilized thought. On the other hand, I knew that nursing homes, ostensibly dedicated to caring, were widely perceived as cold, sterile, and uncaring.

Why?

Tackling this paradox led me toward a new approach to giving care in the nursing home—an approach that recognizes each resident's desire for a life worth living.

LIFE *Worth* LIVING

Introduction

The design, construction, and maintenance of human habitats should be a major focus of nursing home activity in the years to come.

This book is an attack on conventional nursing home practice. I am not interested in hairsplitting disputes over contemporary methods, policies, or procedures. Rather, my concern is with the flawed definition of *caring* that underlies contemporary nursing home care and management.

Current practice in long-term care is based on a confusion of care, treatment, and kindness. Lying at the root of this confusion is the medical model's fixation on diagnosis and treatment. It guarantees that the majority of our resources are spent on the war against disease when, in fact, loneliness, helplessness, and boredom steadily decay our nursing home residents' spirit. A genuine commitment to improving residents' quality of life demands that we correct these problems.

Given the American fascination with scientific solutions to social problems, the surest way to reform nursing homes would be to invent a high-tech, solid-state machine that improves residents' quality of life, while it cuts a nursing home's pharmacy bills in half, reduces the mortality rate by upward of 15 percent, slashes staff turnover by 26 percent, and halves the infection rate.

Just think—a genuine revolution would ensue if this machine were composed of inexpensive, readily available

1

parts and required only routine daily maintenance. Even if such a gizmo cost $300 to $400 per bed to install, it would be considered an incredible bargain.

Is this a fantasy? No. The machine exists and is operating around the clock at scores of nursing homes across the country. The "machine" is a human habitat built from, among other things, the songs of birds, the echoes of children's laughter, and the tender shoots of green, growing plants. We call it the Eden Alternative.

The Eden Alternative is a new way of thinking about nursing homes. It employs the principles of ecology and anthropology in the struggle to improve residents' quality of life. It encourages the leaders of nursing homes to think less like administrators and more like naturalists. Finally, it summons us all to construct vibrant, supple human habitats in which residents can live.

The structure of this new paradigm for long-term care first took shape in 1991 at Chase Memorial Nursing Home, a freestanding, rural, eighty-bed, skilled nursing facility in New Berlin, New York. At Chase we built a habitat that contains over a hundred birds, four dogs, two cats, rabbits, and a flock of laying hens, as well as hundreds of indoor plants and gardens of flowers and vegetables. In an effort to foster a more homelike social environment, we restructured our nursing department and moved aggressively to make children a part of our daily life.

Can this model be replicated? We know it can. At this writing there are more than one hundred "Edenizing" nursing homes in the United States. They will surely develop and extend the methods and insights we developed at Chase Memorial Nursing Home. We contend that the design, construction, and maintenance of human habitats should be a major focus of nursing home activity in the years to come.

This book was written for people who care about nursing homes. It is a guide to the difficult, exhilarating work of moving beyond the status quo. Nursing home residents and their families can use it as an aid in the struggle to promote change. Professionals can use it to transform their facilities into human habitats. But, now, we must begin at the beginning.

Part I

Taking Care

1

The Truth about Nursing Homes

The specter of the nursing home haunts the infirm elderly and their families. They know in their hearts that to enter a nursing home is to take an irreversible step down the path toward disability and death.

Nursing homes are unsettling to most people. Despite the expensive research findings of a large number of gerontologists, volumes of rules and regulations, and the latest medical advances, the specter of the nursing home haunts the infirm elderly and their families. They know in their hearts that to enter a nursing home is to take an irreversible step down the path toward disability and death.

In the past, I avoided contact with nursing homes because practicing medicine in them frustrated and unsettled me. My medical training had led me to think of myself as a master mechanic who happened to specialize in the human body. Like any good mechanic, I was eager to use my new tools and skills. Struggling to keep a worn-out jalopy on the road is drudgery compared with fine-tuning a late-model sports car.

I discovered, however, that this bias against medical practice in the nursing home was nothing more than a specific example of the general perception that nursing homes are mausoleums for the living. What good is treatment for people who cannot be cured? For the first time, I could see that it is the nursing home's equation of care and treatment that makes it such an unpleasant place.

In general, physicians find nursing home work unappealing because they, too, equate giving care with giving treatment; all their training has told them so. Medical treatment can often be both fruitful and rewarding. Still, it is not the same thing as *taking care*.

Taking care is different from providing treatment. It is an act that carries its own demands, challenges, and rewards. Trying to judge care by measuring the number and effectiveness of treatments given is like trying to identify colors with a yardstick.

Unbelievably, for the first time in my career, I was searching for the answer to the question: "What does it mean to *take care* of another person?"

A Recipe for Suffering

Like the physicians who work in them, nursing homes are hobbled by a confusion between care and treatment. This is understandable because, just like their doctors, these homes are reimbursed by a system that applauds care but pays for treatment.

Nursing homes are large and complicated because of the way they are funded. A sizable portion of the money that keeps them afloat comes from health insurance programs such as Medicare and Medicaid. Because these programs have the greatest experience and comfort with hospital-like arrangements, nursing homes devote considerable time and attention to remaining as much like hospitals as possible.

The recent movement away from the term "nursing home" toward the name "long-term care facility" is a good example of this trend. "Long-term care facility" gleams with medical and scientific efficiency, while "nursing home" reminds us of a time when these facilities were boarding houses run by nurses.

In the United States today, the recipe for a nursing home is well defined. Start with one part welfare dollars, three parts health care dollars, and a generous helping of the frail, ill elderly. Blend with a bookshelf of regulations, concrete walls, and shiny floor tile. Season with medical professionals, and bake slowly under the watchful eyes of owners, regulators, and administrators.

I do not fault the reformers of the past half-century who developed this mixture. They simply applied "Sutton's law." During the 1930s, the notorious robber Willie Sutton, when asked why he robbed banks, replied, "Because that's where the money is." Astutely, early advocates for the frail elderly emphasized the reality of disease over the reality of poverty because they knew the real money was to be found in health care, not welfare. The price they paid, however, was to link the dollars that support the continued operation of nursing homes to the medical model of care. Because the money that fuels the engines of nursing homes is the money that flows through the pipelines of health care, those funds must pay for treatment. Reimbursement is based on the variety and number of treatments rendered. As a result, the principles of nursing home care have been derived from the logic of medical science and compounded with institutional bureaucracy. For nursing home residents, life is therapy, and therapy is life.

A Therapeutic Institution

The residents of nursing homes receive too much treatment and too little care. Together with physicians, nursing home leaders share an astonishing inability to define and deliver care that is not derived from medical or allied medical treatment. Those who doubt this assertion should simply ask the nearest available nursing home manager what it means to take care of another human being. This question is usually met with a puzzled expression and a fumbling response. Almost always, the answer is some variation on the "caring is treatment" theme.

Nursing homes are based on specific, fundamental assumptions about the needs and capacities of the frail, ill elderly. Chief among these assumptions is the idea that the residents' most important problems are disease, disability, and decline.

The very soul of the nursing home is dedicated to treating these problems. Members of the professional staff carefully gather information about each resident and apply standard professional knowledge and logic to produce a care plan, which is then carried out by a variety of paraprofessional assistants. In the best nursing homes, these tasks are done efficiently and are spiced with kind words and gestures.

In practice, "care" is defined as the compassionate, comprehensive treatment of the patient. This sounds good—who could object? How could anyone oppose compassionate, comprehensive treatment? In truth, the confusion of care and treatment does great harm to the people who live and work in nursing homes. Nearly two million nursing home residents in the United States spend their lives lashed to an inhumane daily routine. The dominant definition of care flunks the test of common sense.

The nursing home's obsession with therapy makes *taking care* an especially difficult mission. The devotion to treatment is both misguided and deeply entrenched in the nursing home system, in which status is conferred on the basis of professional standing and authority. The fault is not the individual practitioner's, each of whom operates with the best intentions. The problem, rather, lies with the way nursing homes are organized.

Inside the Total Institution

They may have pleasing, serene names like Golden Acres, Meadow Brook, and Oak Hills, but nursing homes are what are known as "total institutions." They have more in common with prisons, reform schools, military boot camps, and cloistered convents than they do with idyllic-sounding retreats. Slick color brochures, honey-tongued narrators, and expensive marketing campaigns do their best to obscure such comparisons, but they do not change the reality.

In the late 1950s, Erving Goffman took a hard look at all types of total institutions. Goffman's research included a year of field work in a mental hospital, and he subsequently published his findings in *Asylums: Essays on the Social Situation of Mental Patients and Other Inmates*. The defining characteristics of the organizations he studied can still be used to identify a total institution.

> A total institution [is] a place of residence where a large number of like situated individuals, cut off from the wider society for an appreciable period of time, together, lead an enclosed, formally administered round of life.[1]

---

[1]Erving Goffman, *Asylums: Essays on the Social Situation of Mental Patients and Other Inmates* (Garden City, NY: Anchor Books, 1961).

Those of us who live in the world outside are able to sleep, play, and work in different places, with different companions, under different authorities, and without an externally imposed overall plan. However, compare that situation with that of the prison inmate, psychiatric patient, or nursing home resident. In the nursing home, all aspects of life are carried out in the same place and under the same single authority. Residents sleep, eat, exercise, and receive treatment in a single building—sometimes even in only one part of a single building—under careful staff supervision. Each component of the resident's daily life takes place in the immediate company of a large group of other residents.

The fundamental rule is that, while their care plans may differ, all nursing home residents are treated alike. Dinner is served at a specified time, and each resident has an assigned place in the dining room. Nursing home residents are no more allowed to eat what they want, where they want, and when they want than prison inmates are allowed to do. Such a degree of freedom would wreak havoc on the institution's routines.

All phases of a resident's day are tightly scheduled with each activity leading, at a prearranged time, to the next. It is understood and accepted that the overall schedule is created and enforced from above. The typical day is so completely managed that most staff members can accurately predict what a particular resident is doing at any time of the day or night. In one nursing home that I know of, the schedule of "large-group activities" has not changed in twenty years. I suspect that this is common.

The activities that comprise the daily life of a nursing home resident are dedicated to providing compassionate, comprehensive treatment. This is the official aim of all nursing homes, and it does not and cannot vary to accommodate any other priorities. While this is certainly better than the penitentiary's goal of punishment and rehabilitation, the fact remains that it's a way of life imposed on all residents, regardless of their wishes.

A gaping social chasm separates staff and residents in the nursing home. The same is true in other total institutions as well. Who would confuse the raw recruit with the drill sergeant, the prisoner with the guard, or the novitiate with the mother superior? In the nursing home, even the elderly volunteers are clearly marked—usually with pink smocks— to ensure that there will be no confusion. The gulf between staff and residents is so wide that even the lowliest employee has power and authority over the most distin- guished resident.

The Problem of Value

If nursing homes were children, their parents would be poorhouses and hospitals. Given that the stated mission of institutional long-term care is to help the frail elderly, many of whom are also poor and sick, this may seem a sensible arrangement. In fact, it is the worst sort of hybrid.

Nursing homes do not fit comfortably into the philoso- phies, standards, or practices of either parent. Clearly, no one would choose to live in a poorhouse or a hospital: long- term care is supposed to be about "homeness," about lead- ing a life worth living.

Despite this disparity, residents and their families can find much to be thankful for in the long campaign to guar- antee a better quality of life for those who live in nursing homes. Before the Great Depression, most of the institu- tionalized elderly were confined along with the "retarded, the insane and immoral."[2] Before the advent of hospital cost controls, it was not uncommon for older people to languish for months or even years in a hospital bed "awaiting nursing home placement."

Are modern nursing homes better than what came before? Yes, but they are still a long way from what they need to be.

Currently we stand on the threshold of a long period of nursing home expansion. As a society, we are going to spend more money on institutional long-term care, we are going to depend on it more, and we are going to expect more from it. Since 1970 we have seen an accelerating demand for nursing home care. During this same period, the per capita cost of providing care for the frail elderly has also risen swiftly (see center-of-book insert figure 1). Before the end of this century, these demographic factors will collide with an increasingly competitive struggle for resources.

We can already see that the victors in this struggle will be those capable of delivering high value at a reasonable cost. As it now stands, nursing homes deliver a low perceived value at a high cost. To make matters worse, this situation is compounded by social trends that are weakening the sense of obligation across the generations. Ultimately, the elderly must depend on this sense of obligation for protection and sustenance.

Can we create a vision of high-value nursing home care that can be delivered at a reasonable cost and can strengthen the connection among generations at the same time? The answer is yes, if we are willing to surrender some long-held

---

[2]Bruce C. Vladeck, *Unloving Care: The Nursing Home Tragedy* (New York: Basic Books, 1980).

assumptions about caring, treatment, and compassion, and to break free from the conventional wisdom that enslaves nursing home practice.

2

The Confusion of Care,
Treatment, and Kindness

*The typical resident of the typical nursing home
is bloated with therapy and starving for care.*

. . . Long ago, a traveler set out across the Sahara Desert, heading north from Timbuktu. Days passed, and he made steady progress on the road to Marrakech. On the eighth day, he encountered a ferocious sandstorm. The wind lashed him mercilessly and confused his sense of direction. When the storm was over, sand dunes stretched in every direction, and the traveler was lost. There was no shade, and his supplies had vanished in the storm. His tongue swelled and his lips cracked, and he cried out for water. Vultures circled slowly overhead. He wandered aimlessly until he fell to his knees, ready to die.

The traveler did not know it, but just over one of the dunes lay the oasis of Kahlid the Kind, who was known as the owner of the purest water and the most generous heart in the desert. Kahlid regularly rode over the dunes in search of the lost and the forsaken. Just as the traveler was about to close his eyes, he heard the sound of a camel. Kahlid lifted the traveler up and rode swiftly home with him.

Kahlid offered the traveler water and he drank gratefully. The traveler drank until his thirst was gone. At last he spoke: "Great is my fortune to have encountered Kahlid the Kind when Death's cold hand was upon my throat."

"It was the will of God that you should live. I am but his poor servant," Kahlid replied. "Now drink more, for truly you have not taken enough."

"I would, but of water I am full," the traveler said. "Now I feel a weakness and a great hunger. Might I have some food?"

"How can you think of food?" Kahlid asked. "It is water you need. Not so long ago you nearly died of thirst. So drink, and drink deeply."

"Kahlid, I am in your debt. But I have taken my fill of water and now I must eat."

"I think the sun has addled your brain, my friend. You must drink more water or Death will claim you yet."

The traveler turned away when Kahlid offered him the ladle. Water spilled on the ground. Convinced that the man was insane, Kahlid swept him up and waded into the spring. He dunked his new friend's head repeatedly. The man choked and fought for air, swallowing great gulps of water. Kahlid was pleased.

The traveler began to weaken. Kahlid redoubled his efforts, holding the man under for longer periods to ensure that he would continue to drink. The traveler's strength eventually waned, and Death took him. He died in Kahlid's warm, powerful embrace.

Tears streaked down the face of Kahlid the Kind. "If only he had drunk a little more, he might have lived!" He buried the man near the oasis. It was not the only body Kahlid had laid to rest there. "Water, they must have water," he muttered as he mounted his camel and headed out into the desert.

✧　　✧　　✧

Nursing home residents are the thirsty travelers of our time. In the past, these residents suffered from a tortuous lack of appropriate medical and supportive treatment. During the 1960s and 1970s, nursing home horror stories were a staple of investigative journalism. Numerous reports documented unsafe and unsanitary living conditions. Furthermore, residents had no solid protection against the physical and psychological abuse to which they were subjected. Even in the better-run homes, the quality and quantity of medical supervision and the number of trained staff were less than they should have been.

Spurred on by books such as Bruce Vladeck's *Unloving Care*, a drive to improve the standards of treatment in nursing homes gained momentum. Federal and state standards were raised, and geriatrics became a legitimate medical subspecialty. The 1987 OBRA (Omnibus Budget Reconciliation Act) regulations enshrined these changes and placed the full weight of the government behind them. This new emphasis on quality led to better performance, and the lot of the nursing home resident was substantially improved.

By the early 1990s, a new era had dawned in nursing homes. Ensuring that residents were receiving the treatment they needed and deserved seemed as good as Kahlid's gift of water to the traveler. The current emphasis on treatment is shared by managers, clinicians, regulators, and third-party payers. Today, the resident's life is analyzed in great detail, dissected and recombined into a treatment plan that defines every hour of every day of his or her life.

While we are all grateful for the work that has "rescued" residents from the neglect of the past, evidence that they are overtreated is everywhere. One vendor pharmacy's survey of twenty-five nursing homes found that, in five of them, residents were prescribed an average of more than six different daily medications. Some nursing homes regularly spend $200 to $300 a month per resident on prescription drugs. Nationwide, more than half the country's 1.7 million nursing home residents receive regular doses of psychotropic medications. This heavy application of prescription drugs would be unhealthy for any population, but it is particularly dangerous for the frail elderly.

Overmedication is not the only problem. Nursing home residents are regularly subjected to unnecessarily restrictive diets that rob them of the pleasure of eating well. In addition, what contemporary nursing home would be complete without the endless round of "activities programs" that often have more to do with meeting the expectations of regulators than serving the true needs of residents? As the therapeutic mentality extends its reach, more and more pieces of a life well lived are taken over and remade into treatments rendered by certified therapists. The pleasure of animal companionship and the enjoyment of children, music, art, movement, and touch are increasingly the focus of professional therapists and their treatment plans.

The typical resident of the typical nursing home is bloated with therapy and starving for care. If I had the authority, I would fine every nursing home that uses the word *care* when it means "treatment." Rightly understood, treatment is the provision of competent, comprehensive therapeutic services. If these activities are flavored with compassion, so much the better. Common sense, on the other hand, tells us that *care* means "helping another to grow."

A father sees that his children are well fed and rested because a full stomach and a good night's sleep are things that enhance a child's ability to grow normally. The father *cares.* Viewed from the skewed perspective of the nursing home, a father would do these things to prevent malnutrition and stave off madness. The father would be giving *treatment.*

If only we could care for nursing home residents the way we care for children. A mother, for example, waits patiently as her toddler dresses because she knows that the child must develop independence. We expect children to grow, and we do everything we can to help them. It's easy to see that the child who is demeaned or made overly dependent is not truly being cared for. Genuine care requires us to recognize within each person the need to grow, the yearning for action, the desire to *do* as well as to *be.* We know this about children. We must realize that nursing home residents also need to grow, and we must care for them in a similar fashion.

Treatment has a place within the scope of care, but it is backstage, in a supportive role. Treatment does not belong where it is always found in the nursing home: soaking up the spotlight. In the context of genuine care, the only reason to offer treatment is when that treatment either helps residents to grow or enlarges their capacity for growth.

Nursing homes err just as Kahlid the Kind did. Kahlid forced his water on a traveler and finally killed him. He treated the traveler's thirst but did not take care of the man. It's the same in the nursing home. We treat the patient's diabetes and congestive heart failure while the person withers from loneliness and boredom. Care that is defined solely as treatment is selfish and expensive, an inadequate substitute for real care. It is as precise and as cold as a surgeon's scalpel.

Three fundamental principles of care must be understood and placed into service if we are ever to achieve dramatic improvements in quality of life for nursing home residents.

Fundamental Principles of Care

First, we must recognize, appreciate, and promote each resident's capacity for growth. This is easy to do for the pleasant women who enliven nursing home bingo games and Bible studies. It is much harder to accept for the severely demented and disabled. The truth is that all human beings retain a capacity for growth, no matter how small, until the last breath is drawn. The nursing home becomes a way station to the grave when we let conventional wisdom obscure every person's need to grow.

I think this point is important, and I regularly attempt to drive it home to the medical students I teach. We assemble in the foyer of the nursing home and take a short, silent walk to a graveyard adjacent to the building. There I give them time to wander among the headstones, to read the names and dates, to think about the people buried there. Then we talk. They begin to see the enormous difference between being dead and being alive and to realize that the people in the nursing home are very much alive. Nursing home residents do not have the functional ability of a vigorous adult, but they are as much alive as anyone on this planet.

Second, our work must be defined by residents' needs and capacities, not by ours. Kahlid the Kind forced water on those he rescued because he had the best source of water in the desert. Had he been a truly caring man, he would have answered the traveler's thirst with water, his hunger with food, and his fatigue with a place to rest. When we look at nursing homes with full-time staff psychiatrists, and find that these institutions tend toward a higher than normal use of psychotropic drugs, we are seeing the shadow of Kahlid the Kind. This is treatment, not care, at work.

Treatment is selfish. Professionals apply diagnoses, treatments, and measurements to their patients. Care is selfless. It is guided by the capacities and needs of the person being cared for.

Third, while treatment can be intermittent and brief, care must be continuous and long lasting. In this light, the words "long-term care" are redundant. The "long-term care" industry continually displays its ignorance of the true nature of care. All real care is long term.

If we are going to be serious about taking care of nursing home residents rather than just treating their ills, many things must change. Foremost must be a new willingness to examine the barriers to growth in nursing homes. We must become expert in those things that diminish and obscure residents' capacity for growth. We must face up to three neglected plagues: loneliness, helplessness, and boredom.

Nursing Home Plagues

While there is a general reluctance to assume that nursing home residents are capable of growing, an even more pernicious blind spot exists in recognizing the barriers that confront the infirm elderly. At first, residents' cognitive and physical deficits seem to be the culprits. After all, these people are old and sick, and they have lost the vigor of youth.

Often I ask the medical students who study at my facility to choose which causes more suffering in a typical nursing home: congestive heart failure or loneliness. They nearly always answer that loneliness is the worse of the two. Then I ask, "What is the most effective treatment for loneliness?" Usually, there is a moment of painful thought before a student suggests that a course of haloperidol or desipramine may do the trick. When I answer that providing companionship is the most fitting response, a small smile of relief spreads across their faces.

"Ah, it was just one of those funny nonmedical questions that Dr. Thomas is always asking."

People suffer when they cannot grow. When we truly care for them, we both remove barriers to their growth and help to enlarge their ability to grow. I understand that this idea lies far afield from the conventional wisdom of nursing home practice. That's the trouble with nursing homes.

The reason loneliness, helplessness, and boredom rage out of control is that they are difficult to define in medical terms. Although they cause the bulk of suffering, their roots cannot be traced back to an imbalance of the metabolism or of the psyche. A survey of the leading geriatric textbooks reveals that loneliness is accorded less than a paragraph at best. Helplessness and boredom are not mentioned at all.

The discovery of blood tests for these plagues would revolutionize nursing home care. Imagine the initial scenes that would follow:

NURSE: "Dr. Good, your patient has a markedly elevated serum loneliness factor. What should we do?"

DOCTOR: "I don't know."

NURSING HOME INSPECTOR: "The blood work shows very high levels of helplessness and boredom. What are you doing about this?"

ADMINISTRATOR: "Uh . . ."

What could the nursing home say? Which department would be responsible for loneliness? Who would take care of boredom? How could helplessness be reduced?

That these tests remain science fiction gives us an important clue to the nature of the problem. While diabetes can be treated by measuring blood glucose levels and injecting appropriate doses of insulin, there will never be a pill for loneliness. The severity of diabetes is unchanged whether a person lives with a loving family or in the most institutional nursing home, but the degree of loneliness depends on the situation. To put it another way, diabetes is a failure of the body system, while loneliness is a failure of the social system. The medical model of treatment works for one but not for the other.

Loneliness, helplessness, and boredom are impervious to the silver bullets of modern medicine. Improvement in these areas must come from changes in the nursing home residents' environment or not at all.

We could perhaps reasonably neglect these problems if they were of little consequence. In the acute-care hospital, for example, people are often troubled by loneliness and boredom, and they commonly succumb to helplessness. Because the goal is the short-term treatment of illness and injury, however, medical treatment is rightly paramount, so there is no clamor to reform hospitals.

The nursing home ought to be different. It should not be a watered-down hospital for hopeless cases, rather it must be "home," or at least as close to "home" as possible.

Like hospitals, nursing homes are currently organized around providing medical and supportive services. Each nursing home must be reformed so the work of eliminating loneliness, helplessness, and boredom is central to its mission. When that happens, all nursing homes will finally be capable of providing genuine long-term care.

3

Nature, Hope,
and Nursing Homes

Healthy natural habitats consist of
rich layers of biological diversity.

Those of us who care about nursing homes recognize the need for bridges to connect current practice with a future that delivers a dramatically improved quality of life for residents. Bridge builders must be well acquainted with both sides of a river before construction begins. Successful nursing home reform requires both a clear understanding of our current shortcomings and a vision of what ought to be.

Regarding our current shortcomings, chapters 1 and 2 outline a critique of the nursing home status quo. Clearly, we place too much emphasis on treatment and too little on helping residents to grow. The major barriers to growth in the nursing home—loneliness, helplessness, and boredom—are three afflictions that account for the bulk of suffering. They are derived, in large part, from the context in which residents lead their lives. Any attempt to overcome these problems must deal directly with the structure and function of the contemporary nursing home.

In the summer of 1991, a group of us at Chase Memorial Nursing Home began to toy with a radically unscientific, nonmedical approach to life for our eighty residents. We could see that the people we cared for were suffering needlessly. How, we asked, can we make Chase Memorial a better place to live? After several rounds of lively debate, we hammered out our answer to this question into the form of a grant proposal. Happily, the New York State Department of Health funded it. We call our approach the Eden Alternative, and for us, it has become a new way of envisioning what a nursing home can be.

The Near Side of the River: Neglected Human Needs

Need for Companionship

Companionship is food and drink for the human spirit. All people, in all cultures, in all of recorded history, have sought the pleasures of companionship and have suffered when it was lacking. Current nursing home practice does not provide residents with the companionship they need. There are activities and treatments, not to mention nonstop "caregiving," but none of these offer real companionship. The situation reminds me of a character in the Bernard Malamud novel *A New Life:* "Levin wanted friendship and got friendliness; he wanted steak and they offered Spam." We need a balm for loneliness.

Need to Care for Others

Human beings find pleasure in caring for others. In fact, this satisfaction has led many of us to work in long-term care. Even though frail people depend on us, they retain the vital human need to give care to others. The sting of requiring constant attention is soothed when a person can give as well as receive care. Cognitive impairment limits the demented resident's ability to take care of others, but it does not erase the need. Helplessness is a dangerous, debilitating condition that can kill as quickly as a cancer or a stroke. We must learn how to prevent its development and to reverse its course.

Need for Variety

Human beings need variety in their surroundings. The practice of leading life completely surrounded by artificial enclosures and routines is a recent and unproven development. Our ancestors, including the frail and elderly, lived close to the rhythms of the natural world. Cycles of change fascinated them and affected their views of daily life.

We can easily find the need for variety and change in ourselves. The thought of being confined to an institution populated solely by the infirm and the staff members who care for them does not fill anyone with pleasure. Nature always mixes growth and decay, youth and age in its habitats. We owe our nursing home residents no less.

The Far Side of the River: The Human Habitat

Deciding to attack loneliness, helplessness, and boredom is one thing—knowing how to go about it is another. We needed a new way of thinking about nursing homes in general before we could begin to transform our own nursing home. Here we were stymied by our training, by our expectations, and by a rigorous adherence to common sense. As we struggled, we recalled the classic story of the boy and the truck.

The driver of a tractor trailer truck was heading down an unfamiliar road when he came to a highway overpass. Unsure whether he could clear it, the driver slowed to a crawl. The roof of his trailer was too high, however, and it became wedged against the bridge's girders. Before long, police and fire crews were on the scene. They scratched their heads, examined the situation and concluded the truck would have to be cut free. Over the frantic objections of the driver, a welder prepared to sever the roof of the trailer. Just then, a curious farmer walked up with his four-year-old son. The police chief explained the situation and what the welder was about to do. When he finished, the boy tugged on his father's pant leg. The men looked down at him with the gentle half-smiles reserved for children. "Daddy, why don't they just let the air out of the tires?" he asked. Their smiles disappeared and they rushed, red-faced, to stop the welder before he began.

Children see things differently. Where we see brooms, they see horses. Where we see tables, they see caves. Where we see sofas, they see ships. The problem for us was that even though we were working hard to be creative, no matter how we looked at Chase, all we could see was a nursing home. We were frustrated because we knew that creating a new activities program or decorating scheme, while easy to do, would not give us the answer we sought.

The breakthrough came when we found a playground for our imaginations. We began to think of our nursing home not as an institution in need of improvement, but as a human habitat. We started to see ourselves not as nursing home managers, but as the creators and sustainers of a habitat. Once established, this point of view made it easy to think about the character and meaning of care. It allowed us to explore concepts and approaches that lie far afield from conventional practice. Suddenly, the craziest ideas and the most arcane fields became useful. Everything from agronomy to child development and from urban planning to zoology became pertinent to our mission of improving our residents' quality of life. Being able to examine the status quo from the human habitat perspective made us feel as though we had solved an ancient riddle.

Rule books and journals were of little use at this point. We found that they were full of advice on how to maintain a status quo we no longer considered valid. Instead, we turned to the natural world and common observations about nature that are readily available. What should our habitat be like? Simply, it would need to be inspired by the natural habitats that surround and nurture us all.

What can we learn from natural habitats? Our planet's record of constructing and maintaining vibrant and vigorous habitats dates back billions of years. As we struggled to transform our conventional nursing home, the wisdom of the natural world guided us every step of the way. We began to compare the characteristics of our setting with those of a successful natural habitat. This comparison laid bare the failings of contemporary nursing home practice.

Healthy natural habitats consist of rich layers of biological diversity. Collecting members of a species in one place, at one time, and for one reason is a uniquely human, highly unnatural development. The human tendency is to favor the monotony of growing a single crop over nature's seemingly aimless patchwork. This preference led nineteenth-century farmers to plow under the American prairie and to plant thousands of square miles of wheat. Still, the most resilient habitats boast huge, nearly uncountable numbers of species. From tropical rain forests to the polar seas, natural habitats demonstrate the durability and adaptability of life. The next time you enter a nursing home, take a page from the naturalist's book and count the number of species you see. The usual nursing home contains less than a handful. There, *Homo sapiens* rules, a lonely sovereign.

31

Ecologically speaking, the nursing home is a wasteland. People often speak of "humanizing" long-term care. This is a mistake. Nursing homes are already far too "humanized." We began to see that our total social institutions strive for complete control over their internal environment. They work hard to drive nature from their midst. This expulsion desiccates the lives of those who live and work there. The trend must be reversed.

Freed from the conventional understanding of what a nursing home should be, we formulated the first principle of the Eden Alternative: *Biological diversity is as good for human habitats as it is for natural habitats.*

Our new commitment quickly led us to question the narrow social purpose of the nursing home. Its singular mission to treat and care for society's frail, infirm elderly stands in marked contrast to the complexity and variety found in true human communities. Unlike institutions, communities are collections of people of all ages and stages who cooperate voluntarily in different ways for different reasons. Whether it's a farming village or an urban neighborhood, a human community is defined by a diverse membership bound together and dedicated to the mutual accomplishment of necessary tasks.

Accordingly, we formulated our second principle: *Social diversity is as important to the nursing home as it is to a true human community.* We began to see how we could create a diverse social environment for the people who live and work with us. Nursing homes must do more than just offer care for residents. They should care for and educate children, celebrate the accomplishments of their members, and become places where food is produced as well as consumed. The more socially diverse they become, the less like institutions they will be.

By this time, ideas were flying fast and furious. We were excited, but could we put these principles to practical use? Again, we turned to the natural world. Together with the land, plants and animals combine to form a whole greater than the sum of its parts. Unless we worked to harmonize the diversity within our habitat, we would create little more than chaos. This new diversity would need to be connected directly to the residents' needs for companionship, for the opportunity to care, and for variety and spontaneity in their surroundings.

We thus arrived at our third principle: *Human habitats must be driven by the same devotion to harmony that enlivens music and nature.* Nursing homes that contain only one species and pursue just one social function are about as interesting as a musical scale with one note. The secret of every successful habitat, we realized, is the development of harmonized diversity.

One reason the Eden Alternative is so exciting is that it encourages us to ask unusual questions. Freed from the medical and administrative model of nursing home life, many happy prospects became apparent. Why shouldn't we have pets here? Why not have birds, dogs, cats, fish, rabbits, and chickens? Why not bring houseplants into our home? Not just a few, but hundreds? And of twenty or thirty different species?

Why not start a summer camp for children? What about an after-school program? Wouldn't it be great to have, along with our on-site child care, a branch of the local school system? Why shouldn't children be an important part of daily life here?

Why settle for a lawn when we could replace it with a lush garden of flowers and vegetables? Why not grace our residents' dinner plates with delicious food grown right outside their windows?

Each of these questions was a sledgehammer blow that destroyed, brick by brick, the walls of the status quo.

4

The First Eden Alternative

*A cornerstone of the Eden Alternative concept
is that residents should have close and continuing
contact with as much of the human habitat
as they choose to embrace.*

Fabricating the Eden Alternative required imagination and the skills of a weaver. The residents' needs—for companionship, for opportunities to give care, and for variety and spontaneity—formed the warp; staff, and regulatory and budget constraints formed the weft. Back and forth the shuttle flew, until a tapestry emerged within our nursing home.

Like a natural habitat, a nursing home habitat gains strength from the richness and complexity of its interactions. As designers, we worked in conjunction with the resident council to select species that seemed to hold the greatest promise. Our "biological diversity is good" principle afforded us a great deal of latitude.

For example, there are more than eighty parakeets, ten finches, two lovebirds, a half-dozen cockatiels, and two canaries living at Chase. We chose to adopt them because they are small, inexpensive, social creatures that live long lives and are well suited to the nursing home environment. Parakeets, in particular, are familiar to many older people. Few human hearts are immune to the effect of a bird's song.

Birds are so ideally suited to the needs and capacities of the frail, institutionalized elderly that I wonder why all nursing homes do not have them.

As all bird fanciers know, parakeets require a location away from drafts and direct sunlight. These conditions vary widely in our nursing home, so we found that we needed a simple way to position the cages without having to drill holes in the wall every time we needed to move them. (Nor could we drop hooks from the concrete ceilings.) We found the solution to this problem in our own maintenance shop.

Our staff designed and manufactured "life poles"—steel pipes fitted with spring-loaded caps and three to four movable arms. The height and number of the arms can be changed easily, without tools, and the pole itself can be stationed at any point in the room.

Life poles are distributed throughout the residents' rooms and support birdcages (90 percent of our residents have birds in their rooms) and a rich variety of houseplants. In fact, we have found that our parakeets do best when their cages are surrounded by plants. The birds are also surrounded by affection.

All our parakeets have been "adopted" and named by residents and staff, and these birds have become an irreplaceable part of our daily lives. Quotations from staff journals help to show this point:

> Gus really enjoys his birds. He listens to their singing and asks if they can have some of his coffee.

> Several times I found Mr. B. standing near his birdcage whistling and talking to his birds.

The residents are really making my job easier; many of them give me a daily report on their birds (e.g., "sings all day," "doesn't eat," "seems perkier").

M.C. went on bird rounds with me today. Usually she sits by the storage room door, watching me come and go, so this morning I asked her if she wanted to go with me. She very enthusiastically agreed, so away we went. As I was feeding and watering, M.C. held the food container for me. I explained each step to her, and when I misted the birds she laughed and laughed.

A.O. watches me while I tend the birds. Now that we have moved the pole into her field of vision, I think she is much more aware of them.

The parakeets are just one piece of the human habitat puzzle, but their presence has done much to fulfill the needs of the people who live and work here. The birds are companions. Many of our least cognitive-impaired residents speak freely and often of their affection for them. We believe that even the most cognitive-impaired residents are aware of the birds' presence and their role.

Many residents are active in the care of their birds. Even those who are physically incapable of feeding and watering them often ask the staff for changes in routine or in the layout of their room in order to make life better for their birds.

Our residents also share their home with two dogs and four cats. The dogs, a retired greyhound racer named Target and a lap-sized, mixed-breed dog named Ginger, have become central features of our habitat.

Target and Ginger are free to roam about at all times. They usually choose to accompany the Eden Alternative staff person responsible for feeding the birds during morning rounds. As a result, the dogs move through all parts of the living quarters, and all residents have the opportunity for daily contact with them.

A cornerstone of the Eden Alternative concept is that residents should have close and continuing contact with as much of the human habitat as they choose to embrace. Many visiting animal programs, while a step in the right direction, actually perpetuate the programmed-activities approach to nursing home life. In those cases, the animal, usually a well-behaved dog, visits the home, and the staff chooses which residents are to be included in the "program." The time, character, location, and duration of the interactions are all determined by responsible staff members.

This approach cannot possibly yield the most valuable benefits of long-term human and animal contact. People outside nursing homes do not interact with animals in this way. What parents would tell their children, "You don't need a dog since you can visit the Johnson's dog for an hour every Saturday"? The real value of the human-animal bond comes from an enduring, caring relationship with a pet.

Toward that end, we also keep four cats, one on each of our units. Like the dogs, the cats move freely within the nursing home. Unlike the dogs, they require almost no staff attention. They choose the time and place of their interaction with humans, the way cats always do.

In order to promote close and continuing contact between residents and cats, our staff developed the "cat pole." Staff members fashioned a shortened fishing pole, a length of yarn, and a bit of catnip into a device that allows residents in wheelchairs to play with the cats. This game brings pleasure to the cats, to the players, and to spectators.

An element of spontaneity arises whenever people live in close association with animals. We found an example of this in the attention our cats pay to the birds, hung tantalizingly out of reach. The cats' fascination has occasioned much comment and many stories of the lengths cats will go "to get a closer look." The animals create happenings, which become stories, which are then passed person-to-person throughout the nursing home.

Together, the birds, cats, dogs, rabbits, and chickens make up the fauna of our human habitat. We have learned that the more diverse and complex a habitat becomes, the greater the potential for meaningful interaction. This is a fancy way of saying that complexity in a habitat, unlike complexity in a bureaucracy, is a good thing.

We also make use of plants inside and outside the building. Indoors, our intent is to subdue the institutional character of the rooms and hallways in which we live and work. Green, growing plants are a powerful means toward that end.

Early in our deliberations on this issue, the head of our maintenance department suggested that we use plastic plants. "They look as real as the real thing. They never need to be repotted or watered, and you can't kill them," he argued. Ultimately we decided against the "plastic plant option" because we had established a firm commitment to increasing real, living biological diversity. Real plants force us to maintain our dedication to the living habitat we are building. Plastic plants would have let us off too easily with little more than a new interior decorating scheme.

Still, we had questions about what kind of plants we should use and where we should obtain them. We called a local firm that leases and maintains plants for businesses and invited its representatives to look at what we were planning to do and to give us a price quote. Their estimate seemed high. How could we carry such an expense after the grant period ended? As usual, money questions forced us to reconsider our goals, but this time we benefited from our second thoughts. Since when, after all, did Nature contract with a horticulturist? It always grows its own.

Families were encouraged to bring plants rather than potted flowers when they visited, and staff members raised money to buy additional plants. As time passed, our plants grew in both size and number. Now they can be found in nearly every room of the building. There are hundreds of vigorous plants and dozens of varieties.

Even so, we're far from finished. We have embarked on an evolutionary process, and evolution takes time, patience, and an openness to new possibilities. Ultimately, the road we travel together is more important than our destination.

Beyond the Walls

Outdoors, we are driven by the same convictions. Having a rural facility, we are blessed with a lawn that would be the envy of many urban facilities. However, the lawn had to go. In order to create biological diversity, we largely replaced the lawn with gardens of flowers and vegetables. Where once the view from our residents' windows was still and green, now residents watch the unfolding of the seasons, the natural drama of birth, growth, fruition, and decay.

Our gardens are designed to be accessible to everyone, both for enjoyment and for work. Nearly every member of the generation that now requires nursing home care can point to a close link with the earth at some time in their childhood or adult lives. The thoughtful use of land is an ancient, universal virtue that should be exercised by every nursing home with arable soil.

Beauty and accessibility are important, but nursing home gardens can also be productive. The provision of truly fresh, homegrown food is an important element of the Eden Alternative. Our dietary staff is inventive and dedicated, but when they're forced to buy the bulk of their fruits and vegetables from California and beyond, variety and freshness suffer. Contrast this with our own harvests of peas, beans, squash, melons, spinach, corn, tomatoes, rhubarb, potatoes, kale, Brussels sprouts, cucumbers, and broccoli. Personal favorites of residents are planted, and unusual varieties are tried. For example, one year it was purple Peruvian potatoes.

Some people may argue that this sort of thing is suited only to a rural facility where many of the residents are retired farmers. That objection actually misses a more fundamental point. We keep the garden because all human beings have a stake in the tilling of the earth. Every ethnic group in every historical age has possessed a rich tradition of agricultural beliefs and practices. The culture of domesticated animals and edible plants is perhaps the oldest, most common denominator that connects us to one another, regardless of age, sex, or creed. We need to make more of these connections, not less.

Another area that nursing homes need to explore more fully is the role of children in everyday life. The prevailing culture has done us all a disservice by isolating children inside school buildings. Once again, a simple look back at thousands of years of history suggests an alternative course. Until recently, children were included in the daily life of their communities. We work to make children an important part of daily life here.

41

Having said that, it must be made clear that simply developing "intergenerational programs" is not enough. Running programs with children, like those with pets, is a staff-directed process. Instead of simply scheduling programs featuring children, we seek to weave their social lives into the fabric of life in the nursing home.

Several years before the formal launching of the Eden Alternative, our administration and board had the foresight to recognize the value of an on-site child-care center. Today, its proximity is extremely useful in ensuring that children and residents experience the benefits of close and continuing contact. Ultimately, I believe the day will come when every nursing home has on-site child care that serves staff, residents, and children.

Preschoolers are not the only group we regularly host. Late afternoon is a slow time at most nursing homes, and many children with working parents have no after-school supervision. Therefore, we created an after-school program that serves both the community and our residents. The program is supported by fees paid by parents, and the children are eager participants.

The after-school program quickly led to the establishment of a summer day camp for schoolchildren. Camp Chase provides parents with high-quality summertime child care, and the children's high spirits blow through the nursing home like fresh air on a warm afternoon. Best of all, like the after-school program, the camp is financed by contributions from parents.

Mixing plants, animals, and gardens with residents and children creates the potential for an enormous number of combinations. While some of these arise spontaneously, others are nurtured by the staff.

Consider, for example, one of the ways in which we bring schoolchildren into our home. We speculated that including children on our staff members' bird rounds would further enliven this part of the daily routine. We thought about including our child-care kids, but they proved to be too young and required too much supervision. Teenage volunteers were another option, but they could not be scheduled in the morning.

In the end, we invited middle-school children. Meetings with administrators at the local school followed; our proposal was received with enthusiasm, since the administrators had been seeking an appropriate avenue of community service for their students.

Now, when an Eden Activities person takes the dogs for their walk on school mornings, he or she stops by the school to pick up a volunteer. The student spends the day at the nursing home, assisting in the care of the plants and animals and visiting the residents. The animals provide a safe middle ground, a focus of attention between young and old that eases many of the difficulties of communication across generations.

Each student records his or her thoughts on the experience in a cumulative diary, which becomes a gift from the students to the residents.

This link between community and nursing home costs no money, and we are grateful to have the assistance of the children. Some of their thoughts on the experience can be found in chapter 10.

Why Change?

Change of any kind is hard work, and sometimes it is not worth the effort. Whenever I become bogged down or frustrated, I think about one of our residents, and his story recharges me.

Mr. L. was admitted to the nursing home just before we began work on the Eden Alternative. I remember greeting him for the first time as I was leaving the building after making rounds. He was walking up to the entrance, his son by his side. Tall but thin, Mr. L. used a cane that he seemed to have more for balance than for support. I told him to make himself at home and that I would see him in the morning for a history and a physical examination. The next day, he told me that his wife of more than sixty years had passed away three months before. He had been living alone and had begun to have a hard time sleeping. He had lost interest in food and found himself depending on his children for more and more of his daily needs. The crisis came when he ran his car into a ditch. His injuries were minor, but he was admitted to the hospital, and arrangements were swiftly made for nursing home placement. As I listened, I wondered how this man had survived at all. Events of the past three months had shattered his world. He had lost his wife, his home, his freedom, and, perhaps worst of all, his sense that his continued existence meant something. The joy of life was gone for him.

His family told me that the police suspected his accident had most likely been a suicide attempt. He had tried to kill himself in order to avoid a life of dependence in a nursing home. With his failure, he found himself truly condemned. He was a resident.

We did our best to treat his depression and to encourage, cajole, and assist him, but nothing seemed to help. First, he gave up on walking. Then he refused to eat and became confined to his bed. At this time, the Eden Alternative began to take root. We offered Mr. L. a pair of parakeets to keep by his bedside. He agreed, with the indifference of a person who knows he will soon be gone.

The changes were subtle at first. Mr. L. would position himself in bed so that he could watch the activities of his new charges. Then he began to offer comments to the people who came in to care for them. These comments grew into bits of advice on what the birds liked and how they seemed to be doing. He was hooked. The parakeets were drawing his spirit slowly back into the realm of the living.

He began eating again, dressing himself, and getting out of his room. The dogs needed a walk every afternoon, and he let us know that he was the man for the job. His condition rapidly improved. His children once again saw the sparkle in his pale blue eyes. Three months later, it was our turn to be sad as we watched him pack his belongings and move back home. The Eden Alternative had saved his life.

Any nursing home that commits itself to the eradication of loneliness, helplessness, and boredom and that begins to build its own habitat, can see these marvelous kinds of stories unfold. All that's required is that staff members steel themselves for the work of change. Standard assumptions about what a nursing home is and what it means to live or work in one must be discarded, and a new vision must be embraced. The Eden Alternative is a new way of thinking about nursing homes—the principles of ecology and anthropology substitute for those of medical science and bureaucracy.

Can we show that the Eden Alternative exerts a measurable impact on the institution and on those who live and work within it? Yes. Our research has led us to hypothesize the existence of an "Eden Alternative Effect." We've identified significant reductions in medication use, mortality, and staff turnover when compared with a control facility. The next four chapters discuss these findings.

5

Medication Reduction

---

*Residents quickly learn that attention comes
hand in hand with medical treatment, and
that a long list of symptoms is the
best guarantee of attention.*

Nursing home residents in the United States are among the most heavily medicated people in the world. If aggressive medical treatment were actually correlated with improved health, the residents would be extraordinarily vigorous. Yet they're not. In fact, when we examine the roots of suffering and disability in the nursing home, it's often difficult to distinguish what is due to disease and what is caused by the treatment of disease.

The Roots of Polypharmacy

By and large, the shared view among residents, their families, and clinicians is that care equals treatment. Health care is, of course, a "sickness" treatment system; the sickest patients receive the lion's share of medical attention. Ordinarily, this paradox is not a problem. Most adults and children only seek medical attention when illnesses interfere with the business of living full, active lives.

Life in a nursing home, however, often establishes a different perspective. Residents quickly learn that attention

47

comes hand in hand with medical treatment, and that a long list of symptoms is the best guarantee of attention. Physicians and nurses reinforce this pattern by responding swiftly and compassionately to "real" medical problems among residents. By equating care with treatment, the medical model of health and illness stacks the deck in favor of polypharmacy (many drugs) and overtreatment.

The struggle for attention is only part of the problem, however. The physical and cultural environment of the nursing home is another major factor in the overuse of medications. We would all be outraged at a health facility that placed its residents in darkened rooms and then prescribed medications to improve their vision. Common sense tells us that these people need light, not drugs. When we place frail, demented, elderly people in long-term care facilities and shut them away from companionship, usefulness, and variety in their daily lives, we too, create a "need" for medications. In this case, major and minor tranquilizers are the drugs of choice. While there are some nursing home residents who truly need and benefit from such medications, the bulk of these drugs are used to compensate for the failings of the institution.

The French have the word *ennui* to describe the very sort of aggravated, dissatisfied boredom that gives rise to most agitation in the nursing home. Residents who bang, pound, yell, and resist care are often just doing what they can to break free of suffocating boredom and isolation. Failing to understand this, the staff members commonly respond to such behavior by campaigning for the prescription of a tranquilizer that will blunt the patient's lack of cooperation. This situation is more dangerous than it seems. As patients become more subdued, they also becomes less active, less able to care for themselves, and more dependent on staff. The risks of infection, of accidents such as falling, and of aspiration rise rapidly for the artificially tranquilized resident. This spiral leads to new diagnoses requiring additional medications and thus sets the stage for an order sheet with a dozen or more routine medications.

The reasons behind this misuse of medications are few in number, but each reason lies close to the heart of the medical model of care. Physicians and other providers have years of training in which prescribing medications is equated with care. When I work with fourth-year medical students in the nursing home, I often ask them whether they have had even one lecture about strategies geared to reducing medications. The answer is always "no."

Patients and their families aid and abet this tendency toward overmedication. They all want the best and most care. What they often get is the best and most pharmacology. Like physicians, patients and their families must be actively educated about the true nature of care. Medical treatment is an important but potentially dangerous component of genuine care. It should be used only when the intervention is likely to relieve suffering or to enlarge the resident's capacity to grow. To do otherwise is to make medical science the master rather than the servant of patient care.

We also need to recognize that the nursing home environment is itself capable of creating the "need" for medications. There is no good reason for 64 percent of all nursing home residents to be maintained on psychotropic medications. The excessive use of psychotropic drugs is itself a condemnation of current nursing home practices. Ultimately, the only way to cut drug use dramatically is to reinvent the nursing home.

Reducing the Use of Medications

The Eden Alternative is a radically nonmedical way of thinking about nursing homes. In practice, it substitutes a holistic understanding of human needs and capacities for a medical model of care driven by diagnosis and therapy. We speculated that such a decisive move away from the medical model would have a significant effect on the use of drugs in the nursing home. Given this hypothesis, we decided to examine the use of medications at Chase Memorial Nursing Home and at a control facility.

We chose a local nursing home that, like Chase, has eighty beds and draws both staff and residents from the same cultural group and geographic area (rural upstate New York). Both homes use the same pharmacy and consulting pharmacists, and all physicians are board certified in either family medicine or internal medicine. In short, you would expect that a similar level of medication use would prevail at each facility.

At the end of the study period (January 1992 to December 1993), we examined the cost of medications per resident, the number of prescriptions per resident, and the average cost per prescription per month for the period. The first and easiest thing to do was to calculate the average cost of medications per resident per day during the study period and then compare the facilities. This analysis revealed that Chase spent $1.44 per resident per day, while the amount for the other home was $2.32 per resident per day. This is an impressive 38 percent difference in the cost, but there's more to the story.

As shown in figure 2 on the center-insert pages, the two nursing homes started with a similar level of medication use.

From that point onward, a significant and growing gap developed. It's not often that you see a health-care-cost trend line sloping downward, particularly when it comes to pharmacy expenditures. This "Eden Alternative Effect" bears closer scrutiny.

The cost of medications per resident per day is actually a composite of the number of prescriptions per resident and the cost per prescription. It could be that the Eden Alternative Effect is due simply to the aggressive substitution of less costly medications, without an associated drop in their use. If this were true, however, we would expect to see a dramatic drop in the average cost per prescription compared with the other home. In fact, the average cost per prescription for Chase was $14.41, while the average cost at the control home was $16.80. This is not a significant difference, and, as center-insert figure 3 shows, the cost per prescription difference explains only a small part of the total cost decline.

The most important factor in the cost decline for medications at Chase is the decrease in the number of prescriptions per resident (center-insert figure 4). The Eden Alternative allowed us to spend less on drugs because we used fewer medications per resident.

We have been able to make dramatic cuts in the use of medications without harming our patients. Of particular interest is the decline in the use of mind- and mood-altering drugs. We believe that pronounced reductions in the use of these medications can be achieved without negative impact on the well-being of residents. In the next chapter, I discuss the reduction in mortality at Chase relative to that in the control facility, but, for now, it's important to note that a careful review of cognitive status, mood scores, behavioral problems, and daily activities demonstrated no decline in function of Chase residents relative to the control residents.

As center-insert figure 5 illustrates, the use of psychotropic drugs in our nursing home was constant until the implementation of the Eden Alternative in 1992. Implementing an enlivened habitat created a large number of new alternatives to the prescription of these medications. In one case, for example, a resident who had been maintained on haloperidol for agitation was taken off the drug when she began to assist with bird rounds. The daily routine with one hundred parakeets did more to soothe the agitation than the medication did.

With respect to national data, we find that the low level of psychotropic medication use made possible by the Eden Alternative stands in marked contrast to the high national and regional levels of use (center-insert figure 6). On the other hand, antidepressants continue to be prescribed at about the same level throughout the country. I think the reason may be that, in the elderly, the need for antidepressants is often biologically determined, and depression is much less amenable to environmental influences than are the agitation and combativeness that so often lead to the use of tranquilizers.

Larger Implications

We have calculated that, if nursing homes in the United States achieved just half the reduction in cost per resident per day that we have realized, it would save our national health care system $1.25 billion a year. However, this is only the beginning. Because we hand out half as many medications as we used to, we require the services of half as many medication nurses. As a result, we have been able to increase the number of employee hours devoted to Eden activities by 60 percent. This shift, in turn, permits us to build an increasingly complex and synergistic habitat for our residents, which further reduces the need for medical treatment.

Federal guidelines express increasing concern over the problem of polypharmacy in the nursing home. Accordingly, there is rising pressure to "do something." I believe that the only way to achieve real, sustainable reductions in the level of medication use is to surrender the nursing home's current exclusive commitment to the medical model of care. The holistic, habitat-inspired Eden Alternative provides us with an opportunity to do more with less. Government and other third-party payers should strive to link decreasing dependence on prescription drugs with increased support for the construction and maintenance of "Edenized" nursing home environments. This approach holds the promise of decreasing overall costs while improving residents' quality of life.

6

Death in the Nursing Home

*It's time we recognize that living
is something more than not dying.*

One of my regular duties as a nursing home physician is the completion of the death certificate. The document includes a section in which I'm asked to specify the cause of death. It's often much harder than it sounds. For one thing, I rarely request an autopsy, and for another, it's not uncommon for a resident to die in his or her sleep for no apparent reason. What, then, can I list? I once wrote that a patient "gave up on living." The health department was not amused. Likewise, "Mr. Jones's time had come" and "Unknown" are not acceptable. The health department needs a "real diagnosis," and I quickly learned that it's easiest just to give them one. This requirement for a medical explanation of death illuminates the extent to which the medical model of treatment shapes our thoughts and practices. In fact, medical science provides little insight into when and why people die.

People who work in nursing homes have seen cases like that of Anna M. Mrs. M. was admitted with a history of severe emphysema and heart disease. Her daughter and her granddaughter were regular and frequent visitors. Despite the severity of her illness, Mrs. M. did well for over a year. Then her son-in-law was transferred to another

55

state by his employer. The goodbyes were tearful, and as soon as they were over, the trouble began. Mrs. M.'s emphysema worsened, and she responded poorly to treatment. Her heart failure, which had been well compensated, worsened and complicated her lung disease. The staff thought she might be depressed, so she was started on an antidepressant. Nothing worked. Less than three months after her daughter's departure, Mrs. M. died. The death certificate read "congestive heart failure," but in the truest human sense, she died of a broken heart. Loneliness kills.

As part of the evaluation of the Eden Alternative, we looked at mortality rates at Chase and at our control facility. As I stated previously, each has eighty skilled nursing facility beds and draws both patients and staff from the same geographic area. Both nursing homes carry an average case mix and neither home has any specialized units. Records from January 1990 to December 1993 were reviewed.

The data were divided into two groups: pre-Eden (the period before implementation of the Eden Alternative) and post-Eden. The first apparent trend was that during the pre-Eden period, mortality rates were rising at both homes. We believe that this rise reflected the trend toward quicker hospital discharge and the associated admission of sicker patients into the nursing homes. We analyzed the frequency of death in the pre-Eden phase at Chase and at the control home. It showed a total of sixty-seven deaths at the control facility and sixty-four at Chase; this difference was not significant. During the eighteen months after full implementation of the Eden Alternative, there were forty-seven deaths at the control nursing home and forty deaths at Chase; in other words, there were 15 percent fewer deaths at Chase. Moreover, the gap between the two grew during the final fifteen months of the study (center-insert figure 7). In 1994 the difference in the mortality rates grew to 25 percent.

How did this happen? Perhaps the residents at Chase were just healthier than the residents at the control home. However, we carefully compared levels of resident function at both homes and found no significant difference during the study period. Perhaps the residents at Chase simply received more comprehensive treatment than the residents at the control facility. Again, this does not appear likely. First, both facilities are staffed by comparably trained physicians. Second, there's a demonstrated decrease in the use of medication by Chase residents during the Eden period.

I believe that the difference in death rates can be traced to the fundamental human need for a reason to live. This view is not a conventionally scientific hypothesis. Human beings are capable of surviving and even flourishing despite hellish conditions when the struggle for existence has meaning for them. On the other hand, those who can find no good reason to fight for their continued existence are easy prey for disease. This is especially true of the frail elderly. In the typical nursing home, such reasons to live are usually confined to the residual contacts with family and community or even simply to a deeply ingrained obstinacy.

Given its core emphasis on the promotion of close, continuing contact with pets, plants, children, and the changing seasons, the Eden Alternative supplies an array of new reasons for living. About halfway through the project, a resident named Mrs. B. gave us a clear indication of the power of the Eden Alternative to reduce nursing home mortality. Although she was afflicted with right-sided weakness and an almost complete inability to speak, Mrs. B. developed a keen interest in her two pet parakeets. To the extent possible, she assisted in their care and spent many hours observing them closely. She made known her wish that the door to her room be kept closed so that her birds "would be safe from the cats." (Note that the cats are declawed and under normal circumstances pose no threat to the birds.)

One morning, I was called to see Mrs. B. because she had developed fever and abdominal pain. I suspected a small bowel obstruction and transferred her to the hospital for a surgical evaluation. There she began to make persistent, emphatic attempts to communicate with the nurses. Unable to determine what she wanted, the hospital staff contacted Chase. It quickly became apparent that Mrs. B. was trying to ask about the welfare of her birds. Were they being taken care of? Was the door to her room kept closed? Once this riddle was solved, Mrs. B. received daily reassurance that "Sweetie and Tweetie" were fine. Her agitation resolved, and she recovered nicely from her bowel obstruction.

I cannot say with certainty that Mrs. B. would have died if she had not come to know, love, and care for her parakeets. What I can say is that her commitment to them engendered within her an intense need *to continue caring* for them, and that this desire in itself is a powerful reason to keep living. I suspect the story of Mrs. B. is repeated in dozens of subtle ways every day in our nursing home. In the end, the sum of these tiny acts of commitment and caring by the people for whom we care has yielded the reduction in mortality.

This conclusion is bolstered by studies that have shown observable changes in the mood and behavior of elderly pet owners.[3] In 1975, for example, Rodger Mugford conducted

---

[3]Alan Beck and Aaron Katcher, *Between Pets and People: The Importance of Animal Companionship* (New York: Putnam, 1983).

a study of people ages seventy-five to eight-one who lived in their own homes. One group was given begonia plants to care for, while the other group was given parakeets. At the end of the study period, the subjects' attitudes toward people and their own psychological well-being were examined. Mugford concluded that the elderly people in the parakeet group had formed a "surprisingly intimate attachment" to the pet birds, even though they had not necessarily indicated a prior interest in birds. Mugford noted that the birds had become so powerful a topic that the caretaking elders talked more about them than about their own medical ailments.

In a similar study conducted in Scotland, researchers gave parakeets to elderly homeowners who had been reluctant to keep their thermostats above 50°F during the winter. These new pet owners were advised that the birds would do poorly if left in cold surroundings. Follow-up studies showed that a majority of these pet owners were willing to increase the temperature in their homes for the benefit of their new pets even when they had been unwilling to do so for their own sake.

It's time we recognize that living is something more than not dying. The richest lives are led by those who are most fully immersed in the work of caring for others. While medical science wages its ultimately futile war on death, the Eden Alternative campaigns for life. Reasons to live are what living is all about.

7

The Administrator as Leader

The best administrators recognize that nursing home care is a collaborative art that all members of the organization and even the community need to play a role in improving.

In the daily operation of a typical nursing home, prudent management clearly holds sway over adventurous leadership. While this cautious style is sufficient for some, the process of "Edenizing" requires both effective management and courageous, committed leadership. After all, no ordinary administrator would consent to plans that would turn a nursing home inside out and upside down at the same time.

The Eden Alternative revolutionized the system of management at Chase while bringing children, animals, and plants into the routine of our daily life. Nursing homes that are Edenizing can expect to experience more change in the first hundred days than most nursing homes see in a decade.

None of this change is possible without leadership. Leaders in long-term care share a perspective that sets them apart from run-of-the-mill administrators and managers. In today's environment, leadership is developed by addressing each of the following issues:

RESPECTING THE INDIVIDUAL—Leaders attune themselves to the experience of living and working in the facility. This sensitivity makes it easier for them to see and respond to the shortcomings of the status quo. Budget reports and survey findings may indicate that the organization is in prime condition, but leaders go beyond those baseline measurements and ask, "What impact are we having on the lives of our residents and employees?"

RECOGNIZING THE HUMAN SPIRIT—Leaders recognize that we must tend to the needs of the human being within the human body. They recognize that damage to the human spirit can be as lethal and as difficult to heal as any physical injury. This point of view doesn't require any particular religious orientation. What it does require is an understanding of long-term care that goes beyond dollar signs and regulations.

CULTIVATING CURIOSITY—Leaders are not afraid to look behind the scenes of their daily operations. While the typical manager works hard to suppress conflict and dissent in favor of an unruffled working environment, leaders ask hard questions that force us to confront blind spots, internal contradictions, and gaps between reality and rhetoric. The most successful leaders spread their commitment to curiosity widely within the organization. Staff, residents, and family members are encouraged to bring forward new ideas that hold promise for improving quality of life.

ACCEPTING THE NEED FOR CONTINUOUS CHANGE—Leaders accept that continuous improvement requires continuous change. The organization that stops innovating, challenging, and evolving immediately falls into a state of decay. Many nursing home managers resist new ideas by pointing to some success in their organization's past, or by saying, "We were the first to . . ." Such evidence of prior flexibility is thought to immunize the home from having to exercise its imagination, grit its teeth, and change again. For true leaders, constant change is understood to be an unwavering requirement of excellence.

DEVELOPING TEAMWORK—Leaders develop teamwork as an organization-wide operating philosophy. I always enjoy being invited to share the Eden Alternative with another nursing home. My heart sinks, however, when after a short tour, I'm ushered into the administrator's office for a private meeting. These folks have plenty to say about their openness and quest for new ideas, but their actions reveal insecurity and an emphasis on control. The best administrators recognize that nursing home care is a collaborative art that all members of the organization and even the community need to play a role in improving. In a nursing home driven by a commitment to teamwork, every effort is made to place decision-making authority with the resident or as close to the resident as possible.

Thinking about Change

Left alone, no object, person, or organization changes trajectory. Change is an electrifying and unnerving process that requires the persistent application of energy. Given this premise, it's easy to see why people are so reluctant to surrender the habits and routines that make their world a comfortable, understandable place in which to live. The problem is that managers share this comfort with the routine. Most nursing home administrators know far less about initiating and sustaining effective change than they do about maintaining the status quo. Leaders, on the other hand, make it their business to challenge conventional practices and worn-out ideas. For administrators who provide both management and leadership, the Eden Alternative offers an excellent opportunity to blend these abilities.

Success depends on recognizing three ingredients of change. First, effective change is always preceded by a growing understanding of the difference between the way things are and the way they ought to be. Sadly, the more successful an organization becomes, the less likely it is to embrace change. The decision to pursue an alternative implies that the status quo is not good enough anymore. Such a judgment can badly bruise sensitive egos. The administrators and managers who built the current operation are the least likely to question the value of what they have accomplished. It's difficult to cast aside your own work and risk what you have achieved on a plan that calls for the radical transformation of a facility. When such a course is taken solely because change holds the promise of improving residents' quality of life, however, the leadership earns a medal of honor.

Second, agents of effective change are able to communicate a clearly defined and apparently reasonable alternative to the status quo. Leaders must always have good answers to the question, "Where are we going and why should we make the trip?" People must understand exactly what is wrong with the way things are and how these shortcomings are to be rectified. Great leaders understand that their vision of a better future must be revealed in words and deeds, again and again. Business improvement programs come and go and never really change an organization, but dedicated leaders who understand where they want to go make all the difference in the world.

Third, effective change is always accompanied by a palpable sense of urgency. Think of the otherwise healthy smoker who visits a doctor's office and is told to quit smoking. The words have little impact. The same advice given to the same patient in the intensive care unit, after a near-fatal heart attack, carries far more weight. Here again, we find an important distinction between the minds of managers and leaders. The typical manager values the smooth operation of the organization over the anxious turbulence of change. Meanwhile, committed leaders realize that even the best-laid plans for improvement will fail unless a sense of urgency exists. If that urgency doesn't exist, then it must be manufactured. Administrators who devote themselves to ambitious plans like the Eden Alternative must learn how to create the urgency that is needed to propel their plans to fruition.

Leading the Charge: Ten Eden Concepts

Nursing homes that commit themselves to Edenizing share a passion for ten fundamental "Eden Principles," listed on the next page. By starting the transformation process with a clear understanding of these principles and a strong commitment to improving residents' quality of life, they are able to slip the bonds of the status quo and explore a wonderful new world. Ultimate success hinges on the leadership's ability to communicate its vision and educate all members of the organization, from the Board of Directors to families, from residents to employees.

Espousing these ideals is easy. The hard part is facing and overcoming the questions, criticisms, and foot-dragging resistance that always make change difficult. The unprepared administrator can quickly be buried by the avalanche: It will never work. . . . It's not my job. . . . We're overworked already. . . . What's wrong with the way we've been doing

The Edenizing Nursing Home

1 Understands that loneliness, helplessness, and boredom account for the bulk of suffering in a typical nursing home.

2 Commits itself to surrendering the institutional point of view and adopts the human habitat model that makes pets, plants, and children the pivots for daily life in the nursing home.

3 Provides easy access to companionship by promoting close and continuing contact between the elements of the human habitat and residents.

4 Provides opportunities to give as well as to receive care by promoting resident participation in the daily round of activities that are necessary to maintain the habitat.

5 Imbues daily life with variety and spontaneity by creating an environment in which unexpected and unpredictable interactions and happenings can take place.

6 De-emphasizes the programmed-activities approach to life and devotes those resources to the maintenance and growth of the habitat.

7 De-emphasizes the role of prescription drugs in the residents' daily life and commits these resources to the maintenance and growth of the habitat.

8 De-emphasizes top-down bureaucratic authority in the home and seeks instead to place the maximum possible decision-making authority either with the residents or in the hands of those closest to the residents.

9 Understands that Edenizing is a process, not a program, and that the habitat, once created, should be helped to grow and to develop.

10 Is blessed with leadership that places the need to improve residents' quality of life over and above the inevitable objections to change. Leadership is the life blood of this process, and nothing can be substituted for it.

things? . . . Just let them try it. . . . If they've got money to do this, why don't they give us all a raise instead?

The most successful Edenizing nursing homes often begin by gathering the members of the management team in weekly meetings that let each manager express doubt and enthusiasm with equal freedom. These meetings allow the group to develop a framework for change that the entire management group can and will support. The consensus sets the stage for a series of facility-wide, mandatory meetings at which the rationale and transformation plan are presented and discussed.

Warning! These meetings can get hot. Some staff members speak in favor of Edenizing, and theirs are soft, pleasing voices. The loudest, angriest words come from those who think the Eden Alternative is hogwash. Objections come in two flavors. Some employees raise valid practical objections. They ask questions about allergies, the threat of injury, and the potential disruption of routines. I've included answers to these kinds of questions in this book. Experience has shown that these exchanges are useful for all parties. Staff members feel better about change when they know that their views will be heard.

Much more difficult to handle are the objections of those who clearly feel threatened by the prospect of change. These comments come from the "I'm already overworked so don't even think about asking me to do one more thing" point of view. The leadership's best response is to require the questioner to frame objections in terms of residents' quality of life. When this is done, the real issue at hand is usually revealed.

Leaders of Edenizing nursing homes have to discuss their vision and their plans freely and openly. They have an obligation to engage others in a discussion of the merits of the Edenizing process. What they cannot do is to allow complaints from those fearing change to derail the process. The entire leadership must make explicit its view that employees who persist in placing their anxieties ahead of the residents' needs should begin looking for a new place to work. The value of such firmness cannot be overstated.

When it becomes clear that the management is lined up solidly behind the Eden Alternative concept, foot dragging and active resistance quickly decline. At Chase, we handled objections during an intensive period of education in the fall of 1991. We enhanced the drama by choosing as the turning point midnight, December 31, 1991. Before that moment, we were a conventional nursing home; afterward, we became an Edenizing one, intent on building a human habitat.

Looking back, we can see how initial resistance and fear melted away and were replaced by affection for the children and animals that shared the home. This habitat, like those in other homes that have followed this path, is deeply rooted; it embraces and is embraced by the residents, their families, and the staff. Today, only a fool would attempt to turn back the clock at Chase. The plants, animals, children, gardens, and team-based management system are part of daily life, and the staff and residents would fight to keep them all.

The Second Revolution

If done correctly, the Edenizing process creates rolling, parallel revolutions. The first, and easiest, transforms the residents' physical surroundings and moves the facility steadily away from the medical model of care. As this happens, the nursing home's rooms and corridors are increasingly enlivened by large numbers of plants, pets, and children. The character of the care given to residents changes as the scope expands to provide them with new opportunities and experiences.

The second revolution transforms the social environment. The physical surroundings in which residents live can be inspected and examined by any interested observer, but their social environment is different. Almost exclusively, it is created from the nature and frequency of contacts with the people who care for them. Often, these contacts take place "out of sight," and there is a widespread understanding that nursing home residents need protection from the arbitrary exercise of staff power. In this regard, the Residents' Rights movement has done much to advance the well-being of nursing home residents.

What the crusade for residents' rights has largely failed to do is ask the crucial question: "Why are nursing home residents in such desperate need of legal protection?" Certainly, the frail and demented elderly are targets of abuse no matter where they live. It is also clear, however, that the federal government has seen fit to provide nursing home residents with a special set of protections. This is because most nursing homes use a management system that differs little from an army regiment's. The military's rigid, hierarchical, command-and-control management structure is well suited to the dynamics of war. Nursing homes, however, are not and should not be fighting wars. Promoting warm, nurturing bonds between the staff and residents while maintaining a paramilitary command structure is like trying to drive a car with flat tires. It can be done, but never well.

Residents deserve the rights and protections they have won. Yet erasing the tradition of paramilitary management has greater potential for improving the substandard quality of their lives than simply enforcing prescribed rights.

The Eden Alternative's Golden Rule of nursing home management is, "Do unto your employees as you would have your employees do unto residents." Tightly restrict workers' daily routines with rules and regulations, and you can expect the same to be visited on residents. Adopt a punitive stance toward mistakes and shortcomings, and residents will suffer under the same lash.

On the other hand, when you expand the decision-making authority of caregivers, you truly "empower" the residents in their charge. Residents will never have more autonomy or self-respect than that which nursing home managers grant their employees.

8

Empowering Employees

*We know of nursing homes that devote
a half-time or even full-time position to scheduling
the nurse aide staff. This is not just a waste
of money, it's a foot on the neck
of the nurse aide.*

Agencies that oversee nursing homes have specific regulations regarding the proper temperature at which facilities must be kept. In New York State, the code requires that nursing homes be maintained at no less than 72°F. This requirement is logical, since residents would suffer if the temperature dropped too low.

It's unfortunate that we do not place a similar emphasis on maintaining the warmth of our residents' social environment. When a resident feels chilly, he or she can seek refuge under a warm blanket or shawl, but there is no shelter from a cold social environment. A recent national survey of nursing homes found that the annual turnover rate for certified nurse aides (CNAs) was 104 percent. This is the social equivalent of leaving the nursing home's doors and windows open on a winter night.

A basic trait of human communities is that their memberships are stable over time. What family, neighborhood, or tribe could have a higher than 100 percent turnover each year and still be worthy of the name? Given the current state of affairs, the name "long-term care" could better be phrased "short-term care given by a succession of strangers."

There are good reasons why CNAs leave employment as often as they do. First, some people embark on nurse aide training without understanding how physically and emotionally demanding the job can be. Most of the hands-on care is provided by the nursing home's staff of nurse aides. If nursing homes were entirely truthful, they would call themselves "nurse aide homes." The nurse aides are the people who feed, wash, dress, toilet, and groom the residents. As a group, they provide these services around the clock every day of the year. I think the job of a CNA is one of the most difficult of entry-level positions, and some people are just not up to its demands.

Second, part of the staff turnover problem is due to the fact that many nurse aides are young people who are not ready to settle in for a decade at any job.

Third, because of the long tradition of high turnover within their staff of nurse aides, administrators have come to regard them as "interchangeable parts." This mentality leads to reliance on expensive agency staffing and an indifferent attitude toward the legitimate concerns of nurse aides.

In the typical nursing home, managing a CNA is not much different from managing an army private. The main difference is that an aide is free to quit the nursing home, whereas the private who "quits" the army is likely to wind up in the stockade. The nurse aide and the private each face a steep, unyielding hierarchy that they have little hope of climbing. In most nursing homes, every aspect of the aide's duties is usually scripted. The work schedule is assembled by superiors, and the daily assignments (i.e., the aide's patients) are most often determined in advance.

The justification for this kind of treatment is usually based on a general lack of confidence in the people who fill these positions. At conference after conference I have asked, "How many of you allow CNAs to make their own work schedules?" While some volunteer that they allow aides to make "requests," I have yet to find a nursing home that hands a blank form at the beginning of the month to the nurse aides—or nurses, for that matter—and receives a completed schedule that can be posted. When I describe our system of self-scheduling, I am greeted with snickers and folded arms.

"That would never work with our CNAs," they say. This belies the interchangeable-parts attitude that fuels staff turnover. These people are correct—self-scheduling will not work in their homes. Yet the fault lies not with the aides but with the management.

A Program of Empowerment

It took time for the CNAs at Chase to learn the skills and judgment required for self-scheduling. At the beginning, we were presented with schedules that were apt to have seven aides on Wednesday and none on Friday. It was tempting to "fix" the schedule ourselves, but, instead, we returned it to the nurse aides and asked them to have another go at it. Round and round it went. After investing time and patience, we now have a CNA staff in control of its own work schedule.

We know of nursing homes that devote a half-time or even full-time position to scheduling the nurse aide staff. This is not just a waste of money, it's a foot on the neck of the nurse aide. After all, competent adults should have at least some control over their schedule. Self-scheduling is a vote of confidence in the nurse aide that, like all such declarations, is repaid many times over.

This move was only the first step in our program of empowerment. CNAs need to organize their work schedule inside the nursing home as well. Before we began the Eden Alternative, aides arrived for work and were given their assignments for the shift. Like aides everywhere, they carried out the duties listed in the order in which they were given. This practice is common because the managers of nursing homes mistakenly believe that they know more than caregivers about the residents' needs.

We have successfully moved to a system in which our nurse aides divide the work among themselves during every shift. The aides have been granted more control over their work and have responded with an increasingly vibrant and durable commitment to providing the best possible care. Naysayers need to understand that this fruit can only be harvested after it has been carefully cultivated.

In order to maximize our gains, we also reformed the nursing department. Before the Eden Alternative, it was organized along conventional lines. Although Chase has just eighty beds, there were three layers of management above the nurse aides. Like most nursing homes, we were hobbled by management conflicts and interdepartmental bickering. The way out of this trap, we found, was to place as much decision-making power as close to the resident as possible. Perhaps not surprisingly, this approach was not warmly received by nursing middle management.

Our reorganization plan, carried out in concert with the implementation of the Eden Alternative, eliminated two layers of management and created four interdependent teams. In our case, one middle manager left immediately, and the other (after serving for six months as a team leader) took a job as a director of nursing at another facility. We were sad to see them leave, of course, but despite the pain of reorganization, the team concept has been a success. The empowerment of the nurse aides and the diffusion of accountability and responsibility have led to a 26 percent decrease in nurse aide turnover compared with the control home. In other words, our facility now loses an average of six fewer aides per year than the control home. We have estimated that each turnover of a nurse aide position costs us about $2,000 in recruitment and training expenses, so decreased turnover saves us about $12,000 a year.

In industry, companies are increasingly revolving around multiple, cross-functional teams that incorporate people with different skills and backgrounds. Nursing homes need to follow this lead. We are sold on the value of the team concept, and now we're moving to expand its scope. Eden Activities people and housekeepers also are to be included as team members. In the years following this experiment, scores of other nursing homes have put these principles into practice. The consensus is that, while the pain is real and the effort constant, dramatic improvements in morale and reductions in turnover are possible. The effort is worthwhile, because reducing staff turnover is one key to improving residents' quality of life.

Lois Griesing: An Eden Supporter

Lois Griesing is a mentor and a friend who has provided me with advice and support that have proven crucial to the development of the Eden Alternative. Hers is an authentic, experienced voice that speaks clearly to the need for change. When we started the project, I was a young family doctor, fresh and untested. She was then, and remains now, a wise leader with decades of experience. The story of the Eden Alternative would not be complete without sharing her views. Now retired, Lois served with distinction as the director of nurses for Chase Memorial Nursing Home. What follows is a conversation we had in which Lois discusses her philosophy.

DR. T.: Lois, I think that people who are interested in the Eden Alternative would like to hear how you got your staff started with team-based empowerment.

L.G.: First of all, I have always believed that management styles have a real impact on residents' quality of life. With Eden we really had a chance to start at square one on this whole problem. As you know, our staff spent many hours looking at reorganization and evaluating our people. We wanted to determine where their expertise was and where they were most comfortable working. We wanted to put the "caring equals helping others grow" equation to work on our own staff.

DR. T.: You wanted to help your staff members grow?

L.G.: Yes, I could see that our people would benefit from being given the power to do their thing. Also, growth builds strength. As we Edenized we found that restructuring boosted our productivity. That allowed staff to free up time and to engage in activities that were outside of their "regular jobs." We felt that we could be active in the Eden program and not jeopardize the quality of life that the residents were already enjoying.

DR. T.: Everyone applauds improved productivity, but for most people improving management means improving control. On the contrary, you've put the responsibility for controlling what is going on here into the hands of your staff.

L.G.: Giving up control means encouraging those people who have a sense of accountability to develop that and to become leaders. Direct supervision is being moved more and more to the peer group. This comes from showing [staff] that they can do it, allowing them to do it, allowing them to make mistakes, and allowing them to become better people for it. We want our people to grow and become better.

Dr. T.: A good example is nurse aides and nurses making their own schedules. I've traveled around the country and have spoken often about self-scheduling and have found many people resisting that idea. How did the practice get started here?

L.G.: Our system of self-scheduling was created by trial and error. In the beginning many nurse aides felt that it [schedule making] was not part of their job. Their attitude was, "Just tell me what to do and I'll do it."

When you teach people the process and give them the responsibility for knowing staffing patterns, things change. They come to understand that if you don't provide for a certain number of working hours per day, per shift, per week, residents are not going to get the care they need. When aides are an important part of the process, they begin to understand that everybody can't have the same day off just because it suits their needs.

They begin to consult with one another on their team, and that's when things start to change. Creating a schedule requires them to work together. They begin to say, "Well, there should be one of us here because otherwise no one will know that Mrs. So-and-So only likes to walk at ten o'clock in the morning, and if you're not there then, she won't walk." They begin to ensure that each team will have an anchor person, and that they're in tune with that person's expertise.

DR. T.: So you're telling me that the aides themselves are aware of the need for an anchor person for their unit.

L.G.: They become aware of the need for consistency. For example, intermittent workers who come into the unit to cover for vacations, time off, or sickness, need extra guidance. When nurse aides understand their role as part of a team, they take that responsibility. They realize that they're important, and it gives them a sense of worth to know that.

DR. T.: It's one thing to tell the nurse aides that they're important, but when you help them develop responsibility for scheduling themselves, you're showing them that they're worthy of a higher degree of respect.

L.G.: *Now* I think that they understand that. But it was certainly difficult getting started. I think it took close to six months before they were comfortable enough saying to their peers, "Well, you've had every Friday off, now I think that we need to share Fridays off." Actually, the new system has helped those people who have always been dominated or directed by the natural leader in the group to take up their own position.

It has also allowed them to take control over their lives. Two of our CNAs have struck up their own job-sharing arrangement. They decided between themselves that "if you're off, I'm on" and vice versa, because on the outside they're baby-sitting for one another.

DR. T.: I remember when we had a director of nurses, a nursing coordinator, nursing supervisor, inservice coordinator, and charge nurses in the facility. Then we made a sudden and dramatic shift, eliminating these positions.

L.G.: The changes certainly didn't come easily. I think with any significant reorganization in management there's pain. It's important that people understand that the change is dedicated to improving resident outcomes.

I think that removing middle management and spreading the accountability out over four teams has proven beneficial for the residents because each team member feels more in tune with those under their care. People have a greater opportunity to have a say in what's going on and see their suggestions acted upon. There are fewer layers to deal with. The decision-making authority is right there. The structure is flat, rather than pyramid-shaped.

You still need someone who accepts ultimate responsibility, but when you put good people into a flattened organization you begin to see the power of peer supervision and peer management. The system works better because it's closer to the needs of the residents.

DR. T.: Recently, Chase has begun to expand the team concept. Now the teams include activities and housekeeping people. The process has really challenged departmental barriers. What are your thoughts on this?

L.G.: If I had the opportunity to go back and start team-building all over again, I truly believe that the teams would have to be interdepartmental from the start. By beginning the process with just the nursing department, we created some long-term problems. Other departments looked in from the outside and continued their old missions, philosophies, and standards. (See pages 82–83.)

What I've seen is that we're now in a stagnant period of team development because we're waiting to incorporate the other departments and waiting for them to catch up with where we are in terms of empowerment and autonomy. So now the team leaders are champing at the bit, ready to get going, and they've been somewhat impatient with the new team members who are two years behind.

We're still working on minimizing interdepartmental barriers, on the concept that it's okay for CNAs to be active in the social life of the resident and that activity staff can indeed feed people. When it comes right down to it, we're all here for the residents, and we can cross-train and cross job description lines if it benefits the residents.

Dr. T.: These ideas are pretty far from conventional thought about nursing homes. You're talking about teams that incorporate people with all kinds of backgrounds and expertise, and operate primarily under peer supervision and coaching by senior management. This is a tremendous contrast with typical nursing homes.

L.G.: Well, it certainly has changed the senior management role. Now we're primarily aware of outcomes and standards. Do our outcomes meet the necessary requirements? If not, why? It really means managing not just the worker but the whole facility. It means understanding that within each team, there are many roads to high-quality outcomes. They can take whatever road is necessary, as long as the results are positive and regulations are complied with. The senior management job description now revolves around improving quality by studying outcomes and providing the training and education people need to do the job right. I think that in the future we'll see more people recognizing that an important route to quality involves removing barriers to pride in workmanship and expecting people to be accountable for the work they do.

DR. T.: How have staff members become involved with the Eden Alternative?

L.G.: I'll tell you one simple thing. Everyone knows that the dogs need to go out, and it doesn't make any difference if it's a housekeeper or a dietary aide or a nurse or a secretary if one of the dogs is standing by the door whimpering. That person won't look for somebody else to do it. They'll let the dog out and they'll let the dog back in again. That's what makes the environment pleasant and the quality of life for our residents better. The birds don't sing until they're uncovered between 7:30 and 8 o'clock in the morning, and we want them singing. It's a sense of knowing what needs to be done and doing it regardless of what your job description might say.

DR. T.: Do you think that attitude has been promoted by the team concept?

L.G.: It has flourished under the team concept and the flattened structure that comes with the teams. That's what allows people to feel that their judgment and their input have value, because you don't have to climb a ladder to be heard.

DR. T.: Lois, you have a nursing home with one hundred birds, two dogs, four cats, kids running around the

Evolution of the Eden Alternative Management Style at Chase Memorial Nursing Home

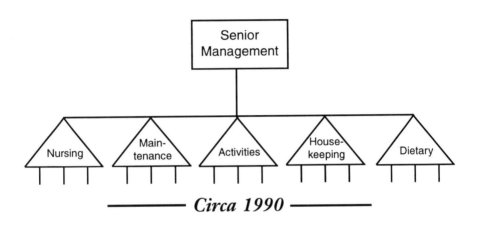

—— Circa 1990 ——

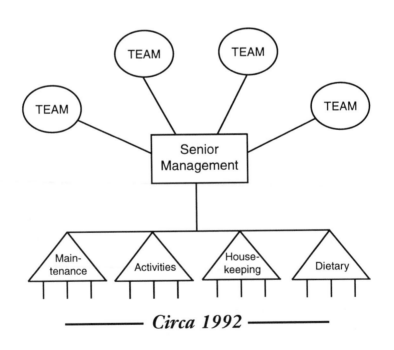

—— Circa 1992 ——

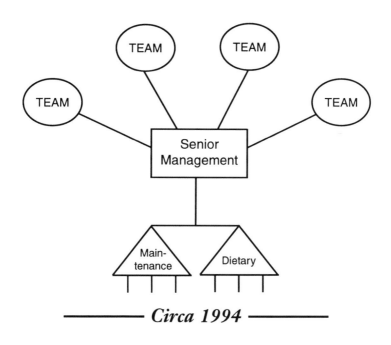

Circa 1994

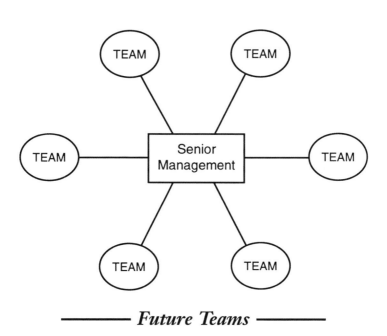

Future Teams

halls—usually every day—and hundreds of plants. How, in your view, has this changed the environment for the residents and staff?

L.G.: I think it's made the place alive, and it's made it happier. Recently, a nurse said to me that she enjoys coming to work because she sees this place as a haven.

DR. T.: One other thing I want to discuss is the question of whether the menagerie of animals and plants and so on is too much.

L.G.: I suppose that it's only too much if you don't like it. But when you enjoy the diversity, you can see the potential for all kinds of beneficial interactions. Diversity leads to increased opportunities for stimulation. Certainly, there is a potential to go overboard in any one area, but I think we've found a comfortable balance at this point. Personally, I would like to see more birds because I love birds, and I think that we could use more bird song here. If you look at a typical nursing home with its bare, sterile environment, and then at ours with all its plants, animals, furniture, children, and gardens, the contrast is stunning.

DR. T.: It's the same thing that makes a patchwork quilt interesting. A quilt of one color and one stitching pattern is practical but unappealing.

L.G.: I think that we still have areas in the home that we could do more with. There are still areas that are barren and sterile, particularly in the areas that don't directly affect the resident.

Other homes that want to try to do this need to start with a circle. The resident belongs in the center and you start to build from there. Begin with the environment that is in direct contact with the resident and then, when that works, widen the circle. If you keep at it, your habitat will keep growing so that eventually it outgrows the walls of the facility and spills onto the outside grounds.

These changes have made our nursing home a more enticing place to visit, and we think it has helped bring outside visitors into our residents' inner circle. I would like to see the whole philosophy extend so far into the community that there are no more boundaries separating the resident from regaining a role as a member of a wider community.

Dr. T.: To what extent has the Eden Alternative impinged on or harmed our residents' rights?

L.G.: I don't think it has impinged on them at all. Residents still have the right not to participate in what is going on around them. None of this is forced on anyone. We respect their right not to participate in the program, not to be part of it. Certainly, we would not force people to do things that they do not want to do.

However, I think that to live means to be exposed to all the different elements of life, and it doesn't make any difference whether you're living in a nursing home and require total assistance with ADLs [activities of daily living].

Dr. T.: Would you do it over again—move to the team concept, build a human habitat, embrace the Eden Alternative—if you knew then what you know now?

L.G.: If I could, I would go back ten years and start this. The benefits to the residents are obvious and they far outweigh

85

the trials and tribulations you must go through in order to get the Eden Alternative off the ground. I think that nursing homes that fail to embrace this approach will find themselves left in the dust of those that do.

The future belongs to those who are adventurous enough and have enough faith in their workers to step out and do it. It just works. Right now, the most important question for other facilities ought to be: "When can we get started?"

Part II
Building Human Habitats

9

The Vision

With this book and a commitment to improving residents' quality of life, you can create an Eden Alternative in your own corner of the world.

Not long ago, I was sitting at a nurses' station, picking through the medical records of a woman I was about to admit to the home, when the elevator doors opened and she appeared before me. Pale, nervous, and surrounded by her adult daughters, she was quickly wheeled to her new room. Nearby, Mattie and Ester, two long-time residents, followed the proceedings with a running commentary.

> MATTIE: "Who's that?"
> ESTER: "Not anyone I know."
> MATTIE: "Never seen her before."
> ESTER: "They're all strangers to me."

Ester's final comment nearly knocked me out of my chair. I tore off a scrap of note paper to record their conversation. "They're all strangers to me." In my mind, that simple sentence encapsulates what a nursing home is and what it should strive not to be.

Only the most wretched among us are compelled to live among strangers. We send criminals to prison because we know they will lose both the freedom of movement and, more painfully, the sense of belonging. Yet even when we remove inmates from their homes, families, and communities, they retain the hope of eventual release and return. What of the frail and elderly—our mothers, husbands, and brothers? They have already surrendered their freedom of movement to age and disease. Admission to a nursing home compounds this loss. It is an exile from which there is neither pardon nor parole.

The Eden Alternative provides protection for those engaged in a life among strangers. No matter how old they are, people need companionship. They also need to be useful and to feel the swirl of life being lived around them. It doesn't matter how pure a nursing home's intentions may be; a life defined by the regimented—and staff-directed—routines of the institution is toxic to the human spirit.

Our program proves that nursing homes can be made into radically different places. At Chase, residents not only live safely among enormous numbers of companion animals but also thrive in their presence. They not only accept close and continuing contact with children but also revel in it. Staff members released from autocratic management practices repay such concrete expressions of confidence with improved morale and lower turnover.

Life among strangers will always be difficult. Accordingly, we have a special obligation to the frail and elderly who undertake its burden. The Eden Alternative can do enormous good, and it needs to be developed, taught, and put into action. If you work in a nursing home, if you regulate nursing homes, or if someone you love lives in a nursing home, you can make a difference. With this book and a commitment to improving residents' quality of life, you can create an Eden Alternative in your own corner of the world.

Changing a Nursing Home

Nursing homes are like locomotives. They're built and operated with the goal of staying on track. The locomotive has no gear shift, steering wheel, or turn signals, only a looming presence and a bellowing horn to warn people to get out of the way. The leadership of a nursing home often acts in much the same fashion. Changing direction is not the average nursing home's strong suit. Leaders are more likely to point with pride at their ability to keep on track and on schedule. By the same token, people often find it difficult to ask for changes that they think are necessary. I remember reading about an airliner that landed in San Francisco Bay, well short of the runway. The crew knew that the plane was off course, but no one was willing to speak to the captain about it. The right things to do are rarely the easiest.

Whether you're a resident, family member, housekeeper, or chief executive officer, you can help others develop what we call the "Eden Alternative Vision." This is the perspective that allows you to view the nursing home as a human habitat. Many efforts have been made to improve the quality of life in nursing homes. What's been missing is a comprehensive prescription for affordable change. People know they want an alternative; they just have not been able to articulate what it should be. Rather than starting from scratch, Eden Alternative Vision builds on the current system and reveals some interesting differences.

For example, the nursing home time clock "looks" different. Conventionally, the time clock is a mechanism for enforcing compliance with an established routine. It gives managers the power to track attendance and tardiness and ensures that a company is getting what it pays for. From the Eden Alternative perspective, however, the time clock is a symbol of the administration's lack of faith in its caregivers. It testifies to the dominance of policy, procedure, and routine. Do you punch a time clock in your home? Whenever managers hold caregivers to a mechanical, down-to-the-minute standard, they condemn residents to an inflexible, daily routine.

Resident empowerment depends almost entirely on management's willingness to empower caregivers. Hard, antiseptic surfaces may demonstrate a devotion to cleanliness, but from the Eden Alternative viewpoint, they also reveal a disregard for the human being's need for close and continuing contact with the living world. Silence is a piercing reminder of the painful absence of children and animals.

I remember receiving a letter from a woman who lived in a nursing home about an hour away from Chase. She had heard of the Eden Alternative and asked whether I would come give a lecture to the staff about what it had to offer. I was teaching a group of medical students at the time, and I asked her whether they could join me. She agreed.

It was clear from the moment we drove up that hope had long ago abandoned this place. The building was run-down, the furnishings antiquated, and the staff dispirited. As I began to talk, I watched the home's administrator closely. First, he shifted uncomfortably on his feet, then he folded his arms and began to frown. He was long gone when I finished and the residents started to ask questions. As we talked, they began to speak freely about their dissatisfactions. On the way home, the students told me that their strongest impression was of staff members rolling their eyes and giggling while the residents spoke. While staff members probably had not been informed about the nature of our visit, it seemed that, along with their leader, they were unable and unwilling to confront their failings.

Fortunately, nursing home professionals are usually much more open to change and to improving the lot of residents.

You can accomplish a great deal by sharing the basic principles of the Eden Alternative with the staff and leadership of a nursing home you care about. Some ideas to get you started are listed in the chart "Ideas to Share" on the following page.

As you attempt to persuade people to join you in creating an Eden Alternative, you will be confronted with objections. While the details may vary, we have found that all objections can be grouped into two broad categories.

"It Isn't Necessary. . . ."

This objection can be raised by both good and bad nursing homes. In the good ones, the administrator and staff are accustomed to walking down the hall and "seeing" a high-quality operation. The problem is that their perspective is derived from conventional wisdom and practice. You need to show these capable and committed people that even though they are doing a good job tending to the residents' bodies, they are not meeting the needs of the people within those bodies. Loneliness, helplessness, and boredom rage as fiercely in good homes as in bad ones. Try to help administrators to see that they can rise above conventional practice and take their organizations to a much higher level of quality.

The bad nursing home is more of a problem. Often there's little pride in reputation and workmanship. The commitment to the resident as a person is perfunctory or missing altogether. Here your options are limited. It becomes essential to organize residents, family members, and staff and to unite them with an impassioned claim for better care. It is terribly easy for homes to meet the minimum regulatory standards and for staff and managers of these facilities to believe that such an effort is sufficient. Do not let bad homes

Ideas to Share

Role	Actions
Family Members and Residents	Organize a discussion group of family members so that you create a joint approach to bringing the Eden Alternative to the home.
	Meet with the administrator and director of nurses and discuss the Eden Alternative with them.
	Prepare a presentation for the home's resident council and learn what residents have to say about these ideas.
Staff Members	Circulate information about the Eden Alternative in your department meetings.
	Seek to create an exploratory group that can give the leadership a report on what the Eden Alternative can do for your facility.
Administration	Build support through educating staff, families, residents, owners, and the board of directors.
Everyone	Do not give up. Transforming an institution as unyielding as a nursing home requires tenacity and a terrific skill for not taking "no" for an answer.

hide behind regulations. Try to get them to acknowledge that caring for the frail elderly is not just a business proposition but a serious, even sacred, obligation. These people need to understand that the Eden Alternative can be an important element in the fulfillment of that obligation. Organize and act as a group. Above all, keep the pressure on.

"It Isn't Feasible. . . ."

Feasibility is a strange, elastic concept. What was unfeasible yesterday can become a necessity today, and what's vital today can easily become unrealistic tomorrow. When you listen to nursing home administrators, owners, and operators talk about the practicality of the Eden Alternative, remember that you are being given their current view of the balance between risk and benefit, opportunity and cost. You can influence the success of your Eden Alternative by working on each of the factors in the chart "Areas to Address" on the next page. Your chances will increase greatly if you address these areas persistently and politely. Try to understand and alleviate the concerns of the nursing home staff while refusing to accept excuses and rationalizations.

Do not fall victim to the harmful fallacy that because your loved one has entered a nursing home, you are no longer capable of questioning and evaluating the care he or she is receiving. I have seen women who spent a decade or more caring for their demented husbands surrender almost immediately to the clinical judgment of the professionals. This is wrong. While we may not understand the details surrounding the treatment of congestive heart failure, we can safely judge the impact of the nursing home on the spirit of our loved ones. I struggled to find a way to illustrate this point until my son Zachary showed me the way.

Areas to Address

Factor	Issues
Risk	Nursing home professionals are extremely wary of anything that may lead to a lawsuit or a regulatory sanction, and with good reason. Help allay their fears by pointing to the success of statewide Eden Alternative programs in Missouri and Texas. Help them reach out to the regulators who oversee such programs so that a dialogue can be established and progress made. All the policies and procedures included in this book are designed to help you minimize these risks.
Benefit	The Edenizing home is far more congenial than the conventional long-term care facility. The Eden Alternative creates opportunities to provide better care, to improve staff morale, and to move decisively away from the medical model of nursing home care.
Opportunity	The Eden Alternative can create a genuine, distinctive difference that sets a facility apart from the crowd. It is a mark of courage and distinction that has a tangible value in the marketplace.
Cost	Remember that the Eden Alternative requires much more change in the heart than in the pocket. The costs are minimal compared with the facility's total budget. In addition, start-up funds and supplies can often be procured from community and philanthropic groups.

The Zachary Test

Our two boys attend the day-care center at Chase and have been a regular part of the Eden Alternative. One day I asked Zachary if he would like to go on a trip with me to a nursing home in a nearby city. I needed to attend a brief meeting there and thought we could enjoy the trip together. This nursing home was, sadly, conventional in all the worst ways. As I drove, the conversation went something like this:

ZACH: When we get there I'm going to play with the kids.
DAD: They don't have any kids there, Zach.
ZACH: Well, I'll play with the dogs then.
DAD: They don't have any dogs.
ZACH: But I can help feed the birds, right?
DAD: Sorry, they don't have any birds.
ZACH: I'll play with the people [residents]. That will be fun.
DAD: Maybe . . . we'll see.
ZACH (in a disappointed voice): Dad, I thought we were going to a nursing home.

Nursing homes, at least Edenized nursing homes, are fun. Perhaps we should apply the "Zachary Test" to each nursing home. Is it full of the vibrancy and vitality that can grab, hold, and satisfy the curiosity of a six-year-old? If not, why?

The home we visited failed the Zachary Test. He clung to me and asked, "Dad, when can we go home?" The facility, which was all spit, polish, and professionalism, had no idea what to do with a child. Zachary was in an alien environment there and felt the strangeness, the pervasive sense of sterile decay.

What about the nursing home you care about? Can it pass the Zachary Test? The Eden Alternative can open up previously undreamed-of avenues of thought and innovation for you. The following chapters show how it can be done.

10

Children

*When they become homemaking organizations,
nursing homes suddenly find themselves capable
of answering their community's needs
for high-quality child care.*

When I had finished my medical training, I moved with my family to a rural area in upstate New York. We bought a piece of land on a hill, pitched a tent, and built a small house. We planted a garden, dug a root cellar, and milked goats twice a day. The house was lit with kerosene lamps and heated with a woodstove. I had done everything I could to eliminate my dependence on outside sources for the shelter, food, clothing, warmth, and entertainment my family needed.

I might have remained alone on my hill with my ax and hoe to this day had I not chosen to become a nursing home doctor. The nursing home shattered my carefully tended illusion that human beings do not need human society to live a good life. The people I cared for laid bare both our common need to belong to a community and the failure of our social institutions to acknowledge and fulfill that need. It also seems that, as a society, we are coming to depend more on social institutions to fulfill the roles family once played.

The more I thought about this situation, the clearer it became that the problem isn't just with nursing homes. I found that many of my concerns about residents' quality of life were echoed in the current thinking about our school systems.

Nursing home residents are isolated from their communities because of age and capabilities. Children are removed from the life of the community for the same reasons. Within the nursing home, administrators seek to boost efficiency by sorting and grouping residents with similar problems. Likewise, the grade system is often more about administration than education. To the extent that the lives of residents and children are defined by their respective institutions, we have failed in the primary mission of educating the young and caring for the old.

Years ago I delivered a public lecture on the future of the family. I believed then that we would witness the development of a cohesive, highly functional family system in the 1990s. I argued that these new, strong families would begin reclaiming the parts of life that have been turned over to professionals and institutions. Encouraged by the rise of home schooling, I also noted the increasing commitment to creating home- and family-care alternatives to nursing homes.

The truth is that the majority of families will come to rely more, not less, on the helping professions and the social institutions they operate. Where I once carried disdain for our "helping" institutions, I now understand that their proper reform is essential to the survival of our society and culture.

Bringing Groups Together

Within 100 yards of our nursing home are an elementary school, a child-care center, and an apartment complex for the elderly. The Eden Alternative Vision suggests that these groups should be closely linked, since each stands to benefit from contact with the other. Even so, contact was intermittent and fragmentary until we began our program.

Think about the day-care kids. For the most part they're in day care because both parents are working and no family elder is willing or able to assume their care. Families are less capable of teaching the young about old age than they used to be. Grandparents and great-grandparents don't live next door anymore and, in fact, may be in apartment complexes for the elderly because there are no local family members to take them in. The options for the nursing home residents are limited even further by memory loss and physical frailty.

Children, however, are good for older people. The hubbub they so naturally create injects vitality into any environment. Their play, laughter, and song are potent medicines for the elderly. The oceans of time and painful need for companionship that most residents possess become assets to children who become a part of daily life in the nursing home. Among older people, nursing home residents have the greatest need for a connection with children, but they are least likely to have access to them.

There are good reasons why we as a society need to support institutional long-term care, day care for children and for the elderly, schools, after-school supervision, summer child care, Head Start, preschool, and public education. However, there's no reason to carry out these programs in isolation. We can all benefit from bringing them together.

Our community, like thousands of others across the country, has a real need for "homeness." The Eden Alternative helps nursing homes make the transition from medically oriented long-term care providers to "homemakers" concerned not only about the frail elderly but about the community as well.

When they become homemaking organizations, nursing homes suddenly find themselves capable of answering their community's needs for high-quality child care. Children can be made a part of life in the nursing home in many ways.

On-Site Child Care

Nursing homes are full of working mothers, many of whom need high-quality child care. The leadership of Chase recognized this need and, to their credit, acted on it. They pursued grant funding to construct a child-care center that accommodates forty children and is adjacent to the nursing home. From the beginning, we fostered a close relationship between kids and residents. Parents who use our child-care center understand and are supportive of the concept.

Child care has been a great success for us, but if you enter this arena, be aware that you take on a whole new set of regulations and regulatory agencies. This burden and high start-up costs are the chief obstacles to overcome. That said, grant money is available for facilities capable of articulating an innovative approach to child care in the nursing home setting. Our start-up costs (building renovations and equipment) for our after-school and summer camp programs were funded with a grant; operating expenses and salaries are covered by parent fees, fund-raising, donations, United States Department of Agriculture (USDA) reimbursement for meals and snacks, and scholarship money from corporate and service organizations.

After-School Care

The number of single-parent and two-working-parent families is growing, and so there is a growing need for after-school supervision. Recognizing this need, we launched an after-school program that also provides child care on school holidays. Not surprisingly, we've linked the children's activities with the life of the nursing home. This interaction improves residents' quality of life by adding another layer of diversity to our habitat. All of this is financed by parent fees.

Sample After-School and Holiday Child-Care Schedule
AFTERNOON

2:30–2:45 Staff meets the children at school, then they walk together to the community center.

2:45–3:15 Attendance, snack, opportunities for socialization.

3:15–4:15 Outdoor play if weather permits, or motor activities such as aerobics or intergenerational activities with residents at Chase.

4:15–6:00 Children are picked up by parents. While waiting, children are given a choice of games, puzzles, arts and crafts, reading, homework help, or music.

Sample Vacation Day Child-Care Schedule
MORNING

5:45–8:30 As they arrive, children are given a choice of quiet activities, such as games or puzzles.

8:30–9:00 Cleanup; breakfast.

9:00–9:15 Large group time, attendance, choice of activities.

9:45–10:30 Large group activities to include music, trips to the library, and intergenerational activities.

10:30–11:30 Outdoor play time or indoor motor activities.

11:30–12:00 Lunch; cleanup.

AFTERNOON

12:00–1:30 Choice of quiet activities such as arts and crafts, games, or puzzles. Rest time for those who require it.

1:30–2:30 Planned small group activities.

2:30–2:45 Snack.

2:45–4:00 Outdoor play, indoor motor or intergenerational activities.

4:00–6:00 Children are picked up by parents. While waiting, children are given a choice of activities such as puzzles, books, arts and crafts, and other diversions.

Summer Camp

Edenizing nursing homes are recognizing the value of operating summer camps for kids. I remember when we started the first one at Chase. The folks at the county office where we had to register were incredulous, to say the least. "You say you're starting a summer camp *at the nursing home?*"

Eden Alternative summer camps welcome school-age children. They benefit from building relationships with staff and residents and from taking part in the care, feeding, and nurturing of the plants and animals. While staff children usually have special preference, the camp makes spaces available to the community as well. It creates a powerful non-monetary benefit, because employees whose children are in the camp enjoy having them close at hand during the summer. Similar to the after-school program, operating costs are funded by parent fees. Edenizing nursing homes are always looking for ways to bring greater diversity to the rounds of daily life, and the camp is an inexpensive way to add yet another dimension to the habitat.

Exchange Student

As mentioned earlier, we now bring a fifth or sixth grader from the local middle school to Chase each school day. Many adults have unpleasant memories of being marched as a group into a nursing home to perform holiday songs. We emphasize the individual, day-long, field-trip approach. The student becomes part of the team taking care of the habitat. The day is spent helping to care for the plants and animals, spending time with the residents, and helping to prepare for upcoming events. We lower anxiety by hosting an orientation picnic that introduces students to the nursing home, explains the Eden Alternative, and describes what their day will be like when their turn comes to join us.

The school administration is often an enthusiastic ally in this undertaking because it offers their students a convenient link to community service. Teachers like it because they can use the students' experiences as the basis for a writing exercise. Students record the events of the day and their thoughts about them. These compositions can make for interesting reading. Excerpts reveal the impact of the experience on kids:

K.C.: I look forward to doing different things when I go. I like the feeling that when I am older, I can live in that nursing home. . . . A lot of people think that a nursing home is just somewhere where you lay in bed all day. Actually, Chase is full of animals, people, and most of all the caring that each nurse and volunteer has to give.

J.W.: It was really inspirational to see those old people having so much fun.

J.C.: Talking with the residents is a great experience, to know what it was like when they were younger how they grew up.

A.C.: Truthfully, I was afraid of it at first because I had never been in a nursing home. We got to play games with the residents and got to fool around with the dogs. I really thought that the residents were pretty funny and nice.

C.S.: My best part was the whole thing!

Community Groups

Nursing homes can effectively host community groups that need a place to meet. We have gone out of our way to entice Cub Scouts, Girl Scouts, and Brownies into our home. Often these groups meet in places like church basements or school cafeterias, cut off from nongroup members. The nursing home is a superior meeting place because it allows direct, immediate contact with those who are dramatically different and can benefit from the attention of young people. No nursing home has to wait to play host. We realized that our Edenized nursing home would make an ideal home base for a 4-H group, so we started one. Most nursing homes can and should host similar groups; or you can consider childbirth classes, senior stretch aerobics, Future Farmers of America, or quilting clubs.

Young Volunteers

Edenizing nursing homes often find themselves facing problems they never considered before. When you work to weave children into the nursing home habitat, they respond with enthusiasm and a desire to do more. I remember arriving to make rounds one Easter week morning early in the life of the Eden Alternative. The halls were swarming with young "volunteers" who wanted to spend the day helping us. Their numbers were overwhelming, their excitement undeniable. While it's true that the plants and animals create many tasks and duties that can be performed by young people, the Eden staff really could not accommodate everyone. It turned out that we had to create a schedule for vacation-time helpers and develop policies to guide their time with us. Samples of these policies and schedules are on the following three pages.

The Unfulfilled Challenge

So what about the connection between the care of the elderly and the education of the young? The natural final step in developing this relationship is the creation of an Eden Alternative School created by and operated within an Edenizing nursing home. As of this writing, I'm not aware of any nursing home that has taken this step.

I dream about it, however.

Somewhere, someone will step out of the shadow of the status quo and create a school that brings young and old together—a school that recognizes that, no matter how young or old, people need to feel at home. Institutions that no longer fill our needs will remain locked in place until we develop something better. This is why I left my mountain and rejoined the world.

Exchange-Student Volunteer Schedule

For students who volunteer as part of a program during school hours

1 The student volunteer will be picked up at approximately 8:15 A.M. and escorted to the nursing home.

2 The student will be assigned to the Eden Activity personnel and will be under their supervision.

3 A definite plan of duties will be presented upon a student's arrival at the nursing home.

4 The student will be instructed in the proper techniques of—

>   interacting with residents,
>   pushing wheelchairs,
>   pushing gerichairs,
>   using the elevator, and
>   caring for and handling animals and birds.

5 The student will be provided with lunch.

6 The student will be escorted back to school.

The above guidelines are to make your time functional and meaningful while you are at Chase. If at any time you have a question, please ask a staff member to assist you. Chase Memorial Nursing Home appreciates your effort to become involved in the life of the nursing home. It takes a special person to work with the elderly population, and for this we thank you.

—The Staff at Chase Memorial Nursing Home

Student Volunteer Policy

For students over the age of twelve who volunteer outside of school hours

1 Student volunteers will be given schedules so that they can be punctual.

2 The student volunteer will be present in the facility only when an Eden Activity staff member is present.

3 The student volunteer must stop at the front desk and sign in and out of the volunteer book.

4 The student will be under the supervision of the Eden Activity personnel.

5 A definite plan of duties will be presented to the student upon arrival.

6 The student is discouraged from eating or snacking with residents. The staff room is available for this purpose; please feel free to use it.

7 The student will be instructed in the proper techniques of—
    interacting with residents,
    pushing wheelchairs,
    pushing gerichairs,
    using the elevator, and
    caring for and handling animals and birds.

8 If a student volunteer is injured while volunteering, this fact should be reported to Eden Activity personnel immediately.

(Continued)

9 If school is closed (e.g., because of snow), the student volunteer should call the nursing home that morning and talk with an Eden Activity person to see if volunteer help is needed.

10 The student will write a brief note describing interactions with residents, if this is indicated.

11 If unable to meet obligations as scheduled, students are asked to call the nursing home.

The above guidelines are to make your time functional and meaningful while you are at Chase. If at any time you have a question, please ask a staff member to assist you. Chase Memorial Nursing Home appreciates your effort to become involved in the life of the nursing home. It takes a special person to work with the elderly population, and for this we thank you.

—The Staff at Chase Memorial Nursing Home

Volunteer _____

Eden Activity Personnel _____

Date _____

11

Dogs

---

*Any dog considered for placement
in a nursing home must have
a "solid gold" temperament.*

Dogs have been our "best friend" for at least three thousand years. Cultures all over the world have strong traditions surrounding the use of dogs as companions, work animals, and guardians of the hearth. At some time in their lives, nearly all nursing home residents have found comfort in the company of a dog. We know of several cases in which frail, elderly people delayed seeking medical treatment out of fear that their dogs would not be properly cared for in their absence. This bond is ancient and powerful.

Many nursing homes are involved in "pet therapy." This often consists of a scheduled visit by dogs from the SPCA, for instance, which is certainly better than having no contact at all with dogs. It's easy to see that residents enjoy these visits and, from the Eden Alternative point of view, it is equally easy to understand that all nursing homes should have dogs living in them. After all, dogs and people have not been visiting each other these last thirty centuries; they have been living together.

When the subject of dogs in nursing homes comes up, I often hear comments like: "We had a dog once, but it just didn't work out." Or, "Sure the residents would like it if we had a dog, but dogs are too much work." These complaints miss the point. Nursing homes are supposed to be good at giving care. Just what are we to think of a home that cannot or will not manage the care of dogs? Should such an institution be trusted with taking care of Mother?

Assuming that a home is willing to shoulder the responsibility that comes with making dogs a part of daily life, some important practical considerations must be addressed, such as the tendency of dogs to become closely attached to the person who feeds, waters, and exercises them. Nursing home dogs are at high risk for becoming security department, maintenance, or administration dogs: fat, pampered, and rarely sighted by a resident.

The Eden Alternative approach provides a solution to this problem. The same people who care for the birds in each resident's room also care for the dogs. As a result, the dogs follow the staff to every corner of the home and cannot help but become regular and warmly received fixtures in the daily routine. This is a good example of the synergy that's created when biological diversity is woven into the fabric of a facility's human habitat.

Selecting Nursing Home Dogs

We believe that one dog for every twenty to forty residents is an appropriate level of "staffing." At Chase, we have two dogs for eighty residents and can easily accommodate two more. There's also no good reason to pay for a fancy pedigree or for rigorous training, each of which can add substantially to the overall cost. In our case, our dogs—Target and Ginger—were put through an extensive and expensive "therapy dog" training course. This was fine, but we intended to use them as pets, not therapists. All a nursing home dog really needs to know is how to sit, stay, and come. Extras, like "roll over" and "shake," are nice but not

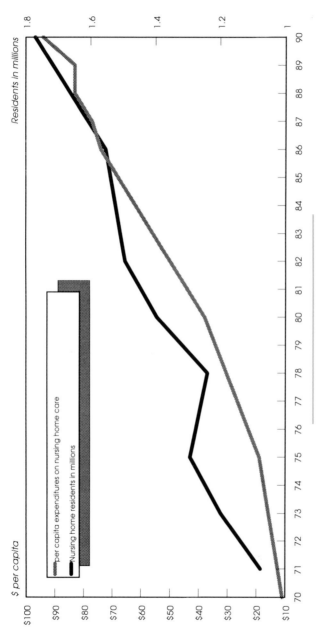

Figure 1

Rising cost and demand for nursing home care in the United States, 1970–1990 *(Source: 1990 U.S. Census Data)*

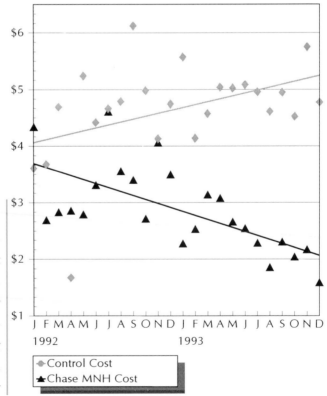

Figure 2

Monthly average drug cost per resident, comparing Chase Memorial Nursing Home and a control facility

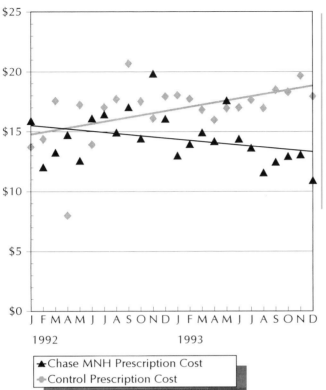

Figure 3

Monthly average cost per prescription, comparing Chase Memorial Nursing Home and a control facility

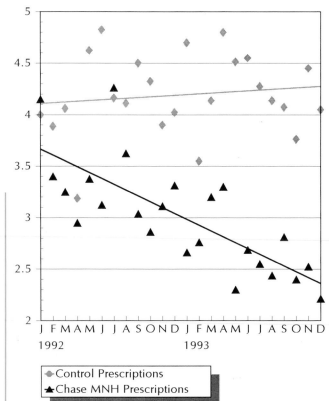

Figure 4

Monthly average number of prescriptions per resident, comparing Chase Memorial Nursing Home and a control facility

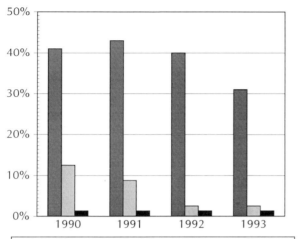

Chart legend:
- ■ % Residents prescribed 1 psychotropic medication
- ▢ % Residents prescribed 2 psychotropic medications
- ■ % Residents prescribed 3 psychotropic medications

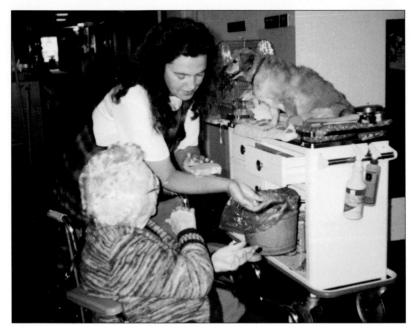

The birdmobile

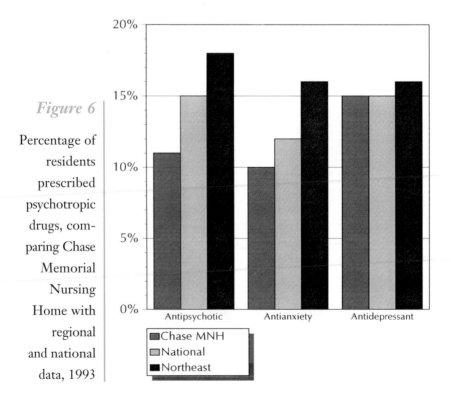

Figure 6

Percentage of
residents
prescribed
psychotropic
drugs, com-
paring Chase
Memorial
Nursing
Home with
regional
and national
data, 1993

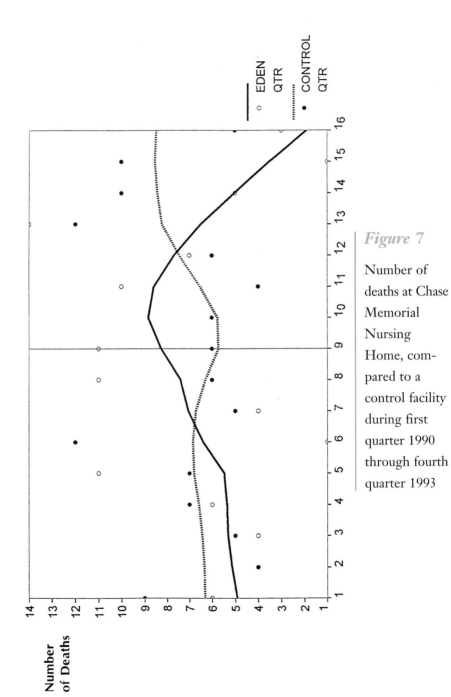

Figure 7

Number of
deaths at Chase
Memorial
Nursing
Home, com-
pared to a
control facility
during first
quarter 1990
through fourth
quarter 1993

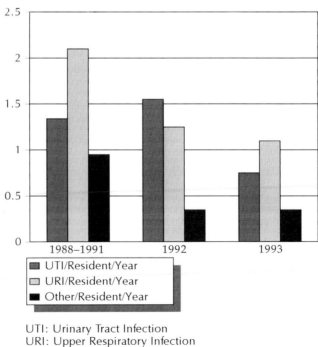

Figure 8

Yearly average number of infections per resident for Chase Memorial Nursing Home in three different periods

UTI: Urinary Tract Infection
URI: Upper Respiratory Infection
Other: Other Infection

essential. Besides, residents get enormous pleasure from teaching the dogs new tricks.

Another key concept of the Eden Alternative is that variety is good. Every nursing home should have more than one dog; it's wise to select different sizes and breeds. For our part, Ginger is a small, long-haired mutt with big brown eyes, while Target is a medium-sized, rail-thin, retired greyhound racer. Despite their reputation as speed demons, greyhounds make nearly ideal nursing home dogs. First of all, they're readily available. Racing greyhounds are so plentiful that most are unfortunately put to death after retirement. The National Greyhound Adoption Program offers information on obtaining a retired racer (usually about three years old at the end of a career). See Pet Resources at the end of this book for a list of greyhound adoption agencies.

Second, greyhounds have a playful, gentle disposition. They stand patiently for grooming and caressing or leap playfully after a toy tossed by a resident in a wheelchair. Finally, their short hair and thin layer of body fat make them ideally suited to the warm, dry environment of the nursing home.

Whatever dog you choose, it pays to consult breeders, animal shelter personnel, veterinarians, and reputable trainers in your area. Every nursing home dog should be professionally examined before a final decision is made.

Adopting a dog that has been a resident's personal pet is always a bad idea. No person or pet could or should be expected to share their special bond with hundreds of strangers.

Placement of dogs in a nursing home will be most successful if the dogs are over one year of age and if you can obtain a detailed history of their lives. This becomes important if there has been past abuse that may make their behavior unpredictable.

Dogs also should be screened with the "Canine Temperament Profile." This can be obtained from the Delta Society (see Pet Resources at the end of the book).

Introducing Dogs into the Nursing Home

When people are admitted to a nursing home, we expect a period of adjustment. Special arrangements are typically made to help the new resident make a smooth transition from his or her previous environment.

Nursing home dogs require the same consideration. "Slow and steady" are the watchwords when bringing dogs in. It is best to start with a series of short visits during which the dogs are kept on leashes. These visits can be gradually lengthened until the dogs are ready to "move in."

Once dogs are situated, the time they spend "out and about" can slowly be increased. At first they need frequent "time outs." A secure wire mesh crate in a room off the beaten path is essential to the mental health of nursing home dogs. They need to be able to escape when feeling overwhelmed. After a couple of months, dogs typically feel comfortable with their surroundings and many new companions. At that point, they can roam the nursing home freely, choosing their schedule and activities. (Our dogs are excluded from food service and preparation areas, however, as well as from medical supply areas.)

Necessary Equipment

A few simple items make it easier to care for nursing home dogs. It pays to invest in stainless steel water bowls and dishes. Plastic is hard to keep clean and odor free, and it cannot stand up to years of use. If your nursing home is carpeted, a tray placed beneath the bowls makes cleanup easier.

Dogs, like residents, need regular exercise. Ambulatory residents often enjoy walking a dog. A retractable leash is easy to use and decreases the risk of entanglement. Many nursing homes find that staff members are also eager to exercise the dog. At Chase, we installed a 100-foot fenced-in run adjacent to our building. This run allows our dogs to enjoy fresh air and exercise, in addition to regular walks, without being accompanied by a staff member. (See the daily schedule on the following page.)

As already mentioned, a crate placed in a quiet, accessible spot inside the home is vital. The crate must be big enough to allow its occupant to turn around and to stand without crouching. The crate should be constructed of stainless steel and should include a removable floor pan or tray. A foam rubber egg crate and an old blanket make a good mattress, but this bedding must be changed and washed regularly.

It also makes sense to invest in basic, professional-quality tools for dog grooming. While our staff are the only ones to use dog toenail clippers, residents regularly take part in brushing and grooming. Some of our brushes have been modified to allow residents with hand weakness and contracture to participate as well.

Veterinary Guidelines for Resident Dogs

The following guidelines are meant to cover most dog situations in nursing homes. If, at any point, there is a question about a dog's health or other problem, a veterinarian should be contacted immediately.

Eden Alternative Dog Schedule

Times are approximate. Once you find a pattern that works, post it for all staff and stick to it. Consistency is important.

MORNING

5:30 Outside to potty in fenced area (maintenance or housekeeping), approximately 10 minutes.

7:00 Outside to dog run for exercise while food is being prepared and cats are being fed; bring in, wipe down if muddy, feed, and give fresh water.

8:15 Take both dogs on leash to pick up student.

8:30 Take on rounds to feed and/or clean birds. Visit with each resident.

10:15 Out to fenced area; break for staff.

10:30 Finish bird rounds; visit with residents.

11:00 Groom (brush teeth, comb or brush hair, etc.); to crates for "time out."

11:15 Residents' lunch begins. Dogs have leisure time (take for walk or put in run area, crates, lounge, etc.)

AFTERNOON AND EVENING

1:00 Visit with residents, review of training, teaching of tricks.

2:45 Take on leashes to return student.

4:00 Feed and give fresh water.

5:30 Outside to fenced area.

6:15 Visit with each resident.

8:00 Outside to fenced area for walk.

11:00 Outdoor rounds with maintenance person.

Temperament

Any dog considered for placement in a nursing home must have a "solid gold" temperament. A dog needs to be well trained in both obedience and good manners, and it must reliably follow all of its commands, including any special training done to customize it for a facility.

The Delta Society Canine Temperament Profile is a good starting point, but I recommend some modifications. During the grooming test, the examiner should check the dog's ears, mouth, and teeth. The hair should be tugged a little (not to hurt, but to be sure that a dog will not react badly if someone does pull on it). The crowd scene should include people with walkers, canes, and wheelchairs, as well as people with abnormal gaits who make strange noises and sudden lurching movements. The distractions should include beepers, metal pans being dropped, and, if possible, a tape of thunder.

Health

All dogs should have a thorough, routine physical examination twice a year. Vaccinations can be given at that time. The minimum vaccination schedule should be a distemper/hepatitis/parainfluenza and parvo/leptospirosis combination vaccine, along with the vaccination for rabies. Ideally, for extra safeguards, I would include the coronavirus and intranasal kennel cough vaccines.

Dogs should have a yearly heartworm blood test and should receive heartworm preventive medication. At this time, I recommend doing a Lyme disease titer preplacement, which would only need to be redone if clinical signs warranted. For information about the Lyme vaccine, consult a veterinarian.

Fecal samples should be routinely checked twice a year, and they should be analyzed immediately if any indication of disease or disorder exists, such as soft or loose stools or blood or mucus in the stools.

Teeth should be clean, and a culture for streptococci should be done during preplacement, with retesting done if indicated. Ears and skin should be free of any external parasites and signs of infection, seborrhea, or allergies.

While it is next to impossible to test for, it helps for nursing home dogs to have an "iron gut," because residents are likely to sneak them inappropriate goodies.

Grooming

Dogs should be groomed on a regular basis. At each grooming, they can be inspected for external parasites, have their nails clipped short, and their anal glands checked.

Daily Care Plan

Every nursing home dog needs a comprehensive "care plan" that includes complete documentation of what is known about the dog's previous health and ownership and an outline of its daily routine. A comprehensive annual examination is necessary, and findings are recorded on a dog's chart. Nursing home dogs also need a regular program of flea treatments.

It makes sense to invest in high-quality, nutritious dog food. We have found that the problem for which our dogs are at greatest risk is obesity. Everyone in the nursing home soon comes to love the dogs, and none of them thinks that this little bit of sandwich or cookie will do any harm. Nursing home dogs should eat only their official rations. It's wise to weigh the dogs regularly and post the results so that problems with overfeeding can be identified quickly and dealt with. One helpful tactic is to distribute a rationed amount of dog biscuits to persistent offenders and to encourage them to use these in place of table scraps. We posted the following Animal Diet Policy:

> Animals within the facility are to be fed only by specified individuals in order to ensure proper control of their diet. If the staff, residents, or families wish to purchase treats for the animals, these must be given to the animal care-taker(s). The animal tender will then distribute the treats to those parties interested in giving them. In this way, the animals' food intake will be well monitored, and hopefully, the problem of obesity can be curtailed.

A Dog's Life

Ecologists who study natural habitats always identify "keystone species" that are essential to the success of the habitat. Without beavers, for example, the web of life that is the beaver pond collapses the first time the dam breaks. It's the same with dogs in the Edenized nursing home.

A word on risk is worthwhile. When I first proposed the Eden Alternative to the Chase Board of Directors, I was questioned closely on the possible risks posed by including dogs in our plan. The concern was raised that dogs would knock residents down or bite a visitor. Wasn't liability an issue? Shouldn't we get a lawyer's opinion before proceeding? To its credit, the Board girded itself and accepted the risks. I believe the members did so because they understood that the only risk-free human environment is the coffin. Our job is to manage risk as well as we can, not to eliminate it. (For more about risks, see chapter 17.)

To date, no injuries have been associated with the dogs in our home. In fact, the dogs have developed a protective sense for our staff and residents. On several occasions, Target, who rarely makes a sound, has barked incessantly and waited beside a fallen resident until help arrived. The night staff has appreciated both dogs' keen sense of the unusual. No strangers are able to approach the building at night without the dogs and staff being well aware of their presence.

We believe that, in the future, the presumption will be that nursing homes should have dogs. Regulators, families, and residents will be looking askance at nursing homes that neglect to make them an important part of life.

12

Cats

---

*Starting with healthy cats is the best way
to avoid trouble down the line, but real success
comes with cats who are also friendly and playful.*

Cats are an essential part of an Edenized nursing home. They are inexpensive, they require little care, and they give so much in so many different ways that it's almost a sin for a nursing home to be without them.

Our four cats—Chase, Sanborne, Pearl, and Eden—are completely at home in our facility. Residents and staff have come to know their moods and habits, and the cats have come to know ours. Our cats make no demands, yet they offer highly dependable affection. They are sleek and playful; it's a pleasure to watch them. They are warm and soft to the touch, and their purrs soothe the soul.

Selecting Cats

Deciding to make cats a part of daily life for residents will soon bring an avalanche of offers to donate "the most adorable cat you've ever seen." Don't allow such generosity to interfere with the task of selecting healthy, well-tempered, mature cats.

The first priority is ensuring that they are healthy and vigorous. Look for the following qualities when selecting your cats: (a) bright, clear eyes without discharge; (b) ear canals free from debris or odor; (c) a sleek, glossy coat showing little or no hair loss or scrubbed areas; (d) pink gums and sharp white teeth; and (e) a firm abdomen. The best bet is to use these criteria to screen the cats you're considering. Then take the finalists to a veterinarian for a complete examination.

Starting with healthy cats is the best way to avoid trouble down the line, but real success comes with cats who are also friendly and playful. The nursing home is no place for a high-strung, nervous feline. The best nursing home cats are alert, active animals that respond to attention and enjoy spending time in a person's lap.

Cats can easily be obtained from animal shelters, veterinarians, breeders, or individual owners. In each case, seek the advice of experienced people to guide you to the best selection. The Feline Temperament Profile is available from the Delta Society and offers additional guidelines (see Pet Resources at the end of the book).

Steps to Success with Cats

NUMBER—You should have a ratio of one cat for every ten to twenty residents. Most nursing homes are large buildings, and a common mistake is to include too few cats. Remember, the goal is to create close and continuing contact between pets and people.

ADULTS—It's wise to avoid kittens. The introduction of cats will be most successful with young, mature animals, at least one year old.

GENDER—In general, female cats are preferable to males. Males, even when neutered, have an unpleasant tendency to "mark" their territory with pungent urine.

SHORT-HAIRED CATS—Short-haired cats are better able than long-haired cats to tolerate the hot, dry environment of a nursing home. There's also less cleanup with short-haired cats.

HISTORY—Just as with dogs, it's best to learn as much as possible about a cat's history. A cat previously owned by a single person, with no other pets, will probably be less sociable than a cat raised with plenty of human and animal contact. All cats should be tested with the Feline Temperament Profile before a decision to adopt is made.

VETERINARY EXAMINATION—All cats must be examined by a veterinarian, spayed or neutered, and declawed before being brought to live in a nursing home. Each cat must receive an annual examination and any vet-recommended vaccinations.

FLEA PROGRAM—Each cat must have a scheduled program of flea treatments. During certain months of the year (usually the late summer and fall), our cats and dogs, like all others, carry fleas. This is not a problem unless the situation goes unchecked and the fleas become too numerous. Although we highly recommend that cats stay inside, dogs must go out for exercise and elimination. As a result, fleas are transferred from the dogs to the cats. We can't hope to eliminate fleas, but we can and do control their numbers and prevent the development of a "flea problem."

LITTER BOX—Given the unfortunate tendency of some nursing home residents to consume nonfood materials, the litter box must have a hood and must be placed in an inconspicuous spot. With these precautions in place, we've never had a problem with residents or visiting children eating cat litter.

FOOD—Use premium, low-ash cat food. Good nutrition is essential to maintain the healthy appearance and high energy levels nursing home cats need. It does not pay to skimp on the quality of food. An ounce of prevention is worth a pound of cheap cat food.

TOYS—When it comes to toys, a few go a long way. We have had great success using old fishing poles with lengths of yarn attached to the ends. Residents in wheelchairs can dangle the yarn in front of the cats and thus play with them. Climbing boxes and balls of foil or yarn are also effective.

ROUTINES—See facing page for our cat schedule and policies.

The cats at Chase have been no problem. Their litter boxes, on the other hand, required some time and experimentation before we completely eliminated difficulties with odor, location, and the litter itself. Feel free to learn from our mistakes.

Steps to Success with Litter Boxes

ACCESSIBILITY—Place the litter box in an area that's always accessible to cats. If the room has a door, it must be kept open at all times. Cats are meticulously clean by nature, so training them to use the litter box is usually easy.

THE BOX—Use a heavy-duty plastic or galvanized steel box with a hood. The hood separates the litter box from the food and water dishes and allows for needed privacy. Put the litter pan inside a clear plastic bag, thus using the bag as a liner. This allows for easy changing with little mess.

THE LITTER—Use "scoopable" litter. We tried numerous types of litter and found that deodorized, scoopable litter saves on time, odor, and cleanup. It may cost a bit more, but in the long run the expenditure is well worth it. Scoop once or twice a day, depending on the number of cats using the

Eden Alternative Cat Schedule and Policies

DAILY ROUTINE

1 Litter boxes
   - **a** Upstairs box must be changed every day.
   - **b** Litter is composed of one-half Quick Dry™ and one-half cat litter.
   - **c** Three scoops per litter box are adequate.
   - **d** Downstairs box is scooped every morning.
   - **e** Both boxes are scooped every afternoon.
   - **f** Cat-litter waste is disposed of in the dumpster on the loading dock.
   - **g** Large plastic bags must be used to line the litter box.

2 Water must be changed twice daily: once in the morning, once in the evening.

3 Food: Shake off top layer and refill with fresh food.

WEEKLY ROUTINE

1 Litter box
   - **a** Downstairs box is changed every Wednesday.
   - **b** Plastic bag is replaced.
   - **c** Waste is disposed of in dumpster.

2 Water/food
   - **a** Bowls are thoroughly washed every Wednesday.
   - **b** Plastic bags under water/food bowls are changed every Wednesday.

MONTHLY ROUTINE

Both litter boxes are emptied and thoroughly washed in the utility room.

box. With scoopable litter, you usually change it only once every two weeks or so.

THE SCOOP—Use a metal scoop rather than a plastic one. We snapped several before we caught on.

QUANTITY—Make sure that the litter is one to two inches deep. Be careful not to under- or overfill. Cats are fussy about their litter box and may stop using it if it does not meet their standards.

CLEANING—When replacing the litter, thoroughly clean and dry the box with a mild soap and disinfectant. Most cats will not use the litter box if it is soiled and smelly. However, a strong disinfectant smell may keep them away as well.

RELOCATION—If you relocate the box for any reason, make sure that the cats know exactly where it is. If you confine them in the room with the box for a few hours, cats will usually catch on.

A final word about cats in the nursing home: yes, they jump up on residents' beds. They even sleep on beds. In presentations about the Eden Alternative, I often show a slide of a cat napping on the bed of a resident who cannot move. Does the resident know the cat is there? We think so. We've heard some fears that cats may harm helpless residents. Properly selected and cared for, cats are safe, sociable companions for even the most disabled persons.

13

Birds

---

*Adding large numbers of birds is a safe,
cost-effective way of providing an opportunity to give
care. Birds provide the variety and spontaneity
so often missing from nursing home life.*

No one is immune to the uplifting effects of birdsong. We all savor those warm spring mornings when we step outside and hear the light, musical conversation of wild birds. Domesticated birds provide their owners with similar pleasures, and those pleasures are compounded by the gift of companionship.

In the early stages of developing the Eden Alternative, we searched for low-cost, easily maintained approaches to enlivening the nursing home environment. We soon began to consider adding birds. They're relatively inexpensive to buy and to feed, and they require little space. Birds are fairly well suited to the temperature and humidity of the average nursing home and can flourish there. Best of all, birds can become true personal pets and companions for the people with whom they live.

We decided to start with one hundred parakeets and to increase from there. We've been able to place a bird or a pair of birds in the room of every resident who wants them. Now the sound of birds drifts up and down the hallways at Chase, reminding us of spring. Staff members visit each bird or pair of birds daily, and depending on their interest and capacity, residents are afforded the opportunity to help tend to them.

Adding large numbers of birds is a safe, cost-effective way of providing an opportunity to give care. Birds provide the variety and spontaneity so often missing from nursing home life. While we must now budget for the labor and supplies needed to maintain our flock, the Eden Alternative has cut the nursing home's pharmacy costs in half. Thus, we can "swing" resources from one cost center to another and live within our budget. The former activities staff has been moved into a new, enhanced "Eden Activities" role. They provide the backbone for all animal care, and they work actively to promote close and continuing contact between residents and the habitat.

Preferred Birds for Birdcages

Parakeets

Parakeets are the world's most popular and abundant pet birds. They're popular because they're easily tamed, friendly, and, under the right conditions, "talkative." As caged birds go, parakeets can tolerate a wide variety of environmental conditions and are willing and successful breeders. Best of all, they're the least expensive of the parrot species.

We started with parakeets because of their nature, low cost, and longevity—the typical life span is ten to twenty years. The best age to purchase them is six to eight weeks after they leave the nest. By this time, they're feeding independently and are ready for ownership. Their attachment to an affectionate human companion can be deep. Parakeets may come to regard their owners as mothers and may spend hours cooing and twittering to them. Veterinarian Dr. Michael Fox notes that "part of this behavior is social and childlike, but some is sexual. Many parakeet owners have become the object of their pets unrequited love."[4] Our residents have confirmed this characteristic.

Cockatiels

Cockatiels are also well suited to the nursing home environment. Larger and more readily handled than parakeets, cockatiels are easy to care for. These birds are terrific entertainers; they have a beautiful whistling song and, like parakeets, live ten to twenty years. Because of their size and expense—they cost a bit more than parakeets—consider using them to provide the spice of variety rather than as the dominant bird species in a nursing home.

Lovebirds

While young, hand-raised lovebirds can be very affectionate; older ones can be difficult to train and handle. Even so, they're beautiful and also usually live ten to twenty years. We have two of these birds at Chase. One, named "Kitten," is bright green with a peach colored face and big black eyes. The other, "Tropical," is bright yellow with a red face. As our staff can attest, these birds are fun, and there's no mistaking their distinctive high-pitched whistles. We handle them frequently; they've been known to escape and fly off down the hall. Far from breaching protocol, these antics enliven our habitat.

Birdcages

SIZE—Birds need physical as well as mental exercise. Cages should be large enough for the wings to spread fully without

---

[4]Michael Fox, V.M.D., *Understand Your Pet: Pet Care and Humane Concerns* (New York: Coward, McCann, 1978).

touching the sides. Length is more important than height. We recommend rectangular or square cages rather than round ones. A bird should be able to fly within its cage.

TOYS—A few toys should be provided for mental stimulation, but don't overcrowd. Mirrors, ladders, swings, and small bells are some favorites. Birds like and need to hear sounds and to see objects.

PERCHES—Perches should not be placed over food or water cups. Droppings in water can cause illness.

COVERS—Cage covers are optional. Some people are faithful about covering their birds in the evening, while others say they never do. In a nursing home, there is activity around the clock. We suggest that you cover the birds to ensure adequate rest time.

PLACEMENT—This issue may not seem especially important, but the health and the well-being of your birds depend on it.

- ✧ The cage should be placed where it is free from drafts.
- ✧ A cage must not be placed over a heater or radiator.
- ✧ The cage should be placed where it can receive some, but not direct, sunlight.
- ✧ The cage should be placed where birds can watch what is going on. They like activity and learn from it as well. Hang a cage at eye level if possible. Birds can become stressed if their cages are too low. This placement also allows for more contact with residents.

The Aviary

We designed and built our own aviary. We simply did not have the money to contract with a company for the sale and maintenance of a fancy birdhouse. We also wanted birds to be companions in the rooms, not just in the common area.

Since the aviary must be cleaned weekly, we took the largest baking sheets available and based the aviary's dimensions on a set of them. We created slots in the floor so trays could slide out for easy cleaning. Whatever the dimensions of your aviary, it should be placed away from drafts and direct sunlight, and it should be covered with wire mesh.

Aviary birds need materials such as twigs, straw, mulch, hair, and thread to construct nests. Make such materials available for them. Aviary birds also need perches and feeding stations, just as birds in cages do.

We stocked the aviary with a pair of canaries, two pairs of zebra finches, and a pair of society finches. The birds have nested and raised their young in it; now we have about sixteen aviary birds. Residents, staff, and visitors have found great pleasure in the sights and sounds created within the aviary.

Preferred Birds for Aviaries

Finches

We find finches to be best suited to large enclosures such as aviaries. They are terrific breeders and are perhaps the easiest way to introduce "birth" into the nursing home habitat. Finches thrive in the flocklike setting of the aviary. These active birds provide a constant source of movement and make a gentle peeping sound. Their life span of roughly five to ten years is less than those of the other species discussed here, however.

Canaries

The canary's sweet song is legendary. As a premier vocalist, the male sings best and most often while trying to attract a mate. These vigorous birds may be placed in spacious cages, but they seem to thrive in the open spaces of an aviary. Canaries are generally healthy, and the male's bright yellow plumage is unmistakable. Their major drawback is that they're expensive to buy. Still, their life span matches that of the parakeet's, and their unique song makes it worthwhile to include at least some canaries in your Eden habitat.

Tips on Buying Birds

Check the condition of birds before you purchase them. If you cannot see them personally for some reason, check references. Look for signs of illness—difficulty breathing, crust around the eyes or beak, puffiness, trembling, or tail bobbing are some of the common signs. Transfer birds during warm weather if possible. If not, make sure they're in insulated crates during transport. Cold drafts can be detrimental.

To Pair or Not to Pair?

There are varying opinions on the subject of pairing birds. Some people feel that a mated bird will not develop affectionate relationships with its owner and that the potential for learning to talk will be reduced. On the other hand, birds are extremely social in their wild state. Some feel that it's wrong to deprive them of their own kind.

At Chase, we've adopted a little of both philosophies. For those residents who rarely interact with their bird, we pair the birds to allow for companionship and an increase in singing. Residents who devote a great deal of time to their pet and who establish a strong bond with it have single birds.

This approach has worked well, but you may have to experiment in your particular setting.

Misting Birds

In the wild, birds receive a soaking when it rains. This helps keep their feathers in good condition, because birds carefully preen themselves after a rain. A bird living indoors —especially in a hot, dry nursing home—will be in a continual state of "soft molt." This means that feathers are continually shedding and being replaced, rather than molting once a season. It's helpful if you mist, not soak, your birds with tepid water once a week. At Chase, we've found that this is a great job for residents and kids. A chemical-free squirt with a misting nozzle, rather than a stream, does the trick.

Diet and Nutrition

Birds expend enormous amounts of energy, and therefore they need a steady supply of high-energy, nutrient-rich food. Birds also need variety. A seed diet alone isn't adequate. In addition to seed, we give our birds a mix of vegetables every three days and an "egg mix" twice a week. The latter is a mixture of eggs, carrots, and teething biscuits. This supplement ensures that they receive adequate levels of vitamin A. Sweet potatoes and peanut butter are good ways to hide medications. The chart on the next page lists other foods our birds receive.

Cautions: (a) Be sure to wash carefully the fruits and vegetables you feed your birds. Just a small amount of chemicals can sicken or kill them. (b) Soft foods spoil. Unused portions must be dumped daily. (c) Some birds raised on seed may be

---

Recommended Food Supplements
for Nursing Home Birds

GRAINS	FRUIT	VEGETABLES
cooked brown rice	apples	broccoli
whole wheat bread	apricots	carrots
	bananas	collard greens
PROTEIN	cantaloupe	corn on the cob
chickpeas	grapes	endive
egg mix	oranges	kale
(raw eggs,		parsley
carrots,		sweet potatoes
teething biscuits)		winter squash
peanuts		

---

reluctant to try unfamiliar foods. Ask your veterinarian for suggestions.

PELLETS—Look into using bird pellets. They are free of dust and hulls and are available in medicated form.

MINERAL ATTACHMENTS—Cuttlebones, white oyster shell, and mineral blocks are good sources of calcium and other minerals. They are helpful beak conditioners as well. Make sure they're securely fastened to the cage near a perch.

GRIT—There are varying opinions on using grit. We believe that if an adequate diet is provided with a variety of fruits and vegetables, there's no need for grit.

The Birdmobile

All nursing homes have medication carts. In the world of the Eden Alternative, the birdmobile fills that role. When we first began, we ran smack dab into a major logistical problem. Every day, we struggled to get the necessary bird-seed, vitamins, egg mixture, and water to all the birds in our more than sixty cages. We needed to maneuver our supplies quickly, and the gurney we had pressed into service was more trouble than it was worth. My wife, Judy, was heading up the implementation of the project, and she let it be known that something had to be done.

Fortunately, we were able to persuade a local hospital to donate a surplus medication cart, and the first birdmobile was created. Its effect is magical. The birdmobile (shown above center-insert figure 6) is taken on rounds according to the needs of the birds and their owners. It is as free from the medical model of care as anything in the nursing home. Because the cart is equipped with dog and cat treats, those animals are often found trailing in its wake. Because we have involved children so heavily in the care of our animals, there's often a youngster or two nearby, helping out. Naturally, residents gravitate to the birdmobile when it's in their vicinity. It becomes a mobile, rolling social occasion that also happens to fulfill an important logistical need. Best of all, it has nothing to do with illness and treatment but carries a message of life and hope.

Judy created the first birdmobile and put in many hours behind it. When we became involved in helping other nursing homes Edenize, she volunteered to search an abandoned state mental hospital for surplus medication carts. She tells of wandering the spooky, echoing hallways in search of carts that could become birdmobiles. From her trips came what we and others have now—drug dispensers transformed into sparks of the human habitat.

Over time, we have developed guidelines and schedules (pages 136–137) for bird care that have served us well.

Eden Alternative Pet Bird Guidelines

1 Never place a bird by a window, because drafts or direct sunlight can be detrimental.

2 Never position a bird directly over a heater.

3 Do not use string or other materials to tie the doors of birdcages.

4 Never give human food (e.g., chocolate or potato chips) to birds.

5 If water is spilled on the floor of a cage, change the paper and dry the floor.

6 If birds get out of a cage, always use a glove or, if necessary, a towel to handle them. Birds bite.

7 Report to the team leader immediately any injury caused to a bird or received from a bird.

8 Always spray residents' sinks with a disinfectant after cage-cleaning procedures.

9 Always wipe up any spilled water or seed after feeding and cleaning procedures.

10 Keep all bird supplies in an appropriate storage area for daily use.

11 Store large quantities of bird food outside.

Eden Alternative Pet Bird Schedule

Daily Routine

1 Give all birds fresh food and water every day.

   a Dump water.

   b Rinse container thoroughly.

   c Replace with fresh, cool water.

   d Shake top layer of seed into garbage.

   e Replace with fresh seed.

2 Change paper daily.

3 Check for illness while changing food and water. Signs are as follows:

   a Shivering

   b Tail bobbing up or down

   c Crusty or runny eyes

   d Ruffled feathers

(If such a sign is seen, administer the appropriate medication or place in bird hospital.)

4 Mist with warm water using spray bottle.

5 Give vegetables and vitamin supplements daily.

Weekly Routine

Clean cages. Every Thursday, cages on the first floor are thoroughly cleaned. Floors of the building are alternated each week.

1 Scrub bottom of cage with hot water.

2 Scrub dishes with hot water.

3 Provide fresh food and water.

4 Change paper.

5 Wash out sinks with disinfectant.

6 Wipe floors of any water.

14
Other Animals

*Nursing homes should be places for birth
as well as death, so we've been delighted by
the stir created by a litter of infant rabbits.*

Animals adopted by nursing homes should have three essential features. They must be relatively easy to obtain, train, and retain; they must be healthy and well-tempered; and they must be capable of flourishing in the nursing home environment.

Dogs, cats, and birds have received the greatest amount of our attention because we've found them to be the most useful. Still, there are other suitable species, including rabbits, chicken, and fish.

Rabbits

Rabbits have an average life expectancy of five to ten years. They can be kept inside or outside a nursing home and trained to use a litter box.

The proper cage size varies with the size of the rabbit. All housing for nursing home rabbits should be equipped with two compartments: one with plenty of bedding and another that can serve as a nesting box. The nesting box should have good ventilation and be dark and quiet. A wire mesh floor allows droppings to fall into a collecting pan below. This floor should be strewn with hay, because a wire cage bottom can harm a rabbit's hind feet. Conversely, you can place a square of plywood on the wire for a "sitting spot."

Food dishes should be of the "hanging type" or have a wide base to prevent them from tipping; many people use the heavy ceramic bowls sold at feed stores. Be sure to choose an inverted gravity water bottle, too.

Local rabbit experts can help you select a proper diet that suits the needs of your rabbits. You can use rabbit pellets or feed them a combination of grains and fresh greens. Greens are rabbits' natural food.

Rabbits need to be handled if they're to remain sociable. Like residents, they also benefit from close and continuing contact. The decision where to house them should be driven by considerations of space and the need of residents to have easy access to these animals.

As mentioned, rabbits can be litter trained. Our child-care center features a litter-trained rabbit named Mr. Puffy. The training technique for introducing rabbits to the litter box is the same as for cats: put the rabbit in the litter box and allow it to scratch. Your rabbit will get the idea.

Nursing homes should be places for birth as well as death, so we've been delighted by the stir created by a litter of infant rabbits. Breeding rabbits is as easy as it sounds, but there are some important things to think about. The best bet is to refrain from breeding them until you are clear about what will become of the kits when full-grown. Seek the counsel of a person knowledgeable about managing rabbit reproduction. Start by asking your residents; chances are, someone raised rabbits.

Chickens

What sound evokes memories of home for many nursing home residents? A rooster's crow. If you have room for a flock of chickens, this is a good investment for a couple of reasons. Their eggs can be used to feed your pet birds (see chapter 13). Also, chicken manure is high in nitrogen and provides a natural fertilizer for your lawn or garden, especially when you allow chickens to run all over the area.

This is how we accomplished that: we built a portable chicken run called a "chicken tractor." We made a lightweight A-frame, eight feet long by four feet wide with a door at one end, and covered it with chicken wire. The chickens were in this pen for three days, foraging and cultivating the soil. Then we picked up the "tractor" and moved it to another part of the lawn or garden.

We did have to make a modification because wild animals dug underneath the "chicken tractor" at night and stole the chickens. We put the chickens back in their house at night.

Fish

We decided not to make fish an important part of our habitat because it seemed to us that opportunities are limited for contact between them and people. That does not, however, mean that it can't or shouldn't be done. The following are a few considerations for anyone who wants to introduce fish into a nursing home.

Vision is the only means of contact between residents and fish; since many residents have impaired vision, use large, colorful tropical fish in your aquarium.

The tank should be as large as possible, given the money and space you have to work with. A general guideline is to stock the tank with an average of one inch of fish for every gallon of water it holds.

Basic start-up equipment includes an aeration device and filter; a thermostatically controlled heater; a source of light that can help illuminate the fish for residents; and sand, gravel, vegetation, and "toys." Any fish tank located in a nursing home should have a cover.

The tank should be placed in an area where groups of residents frequently spend idle time. Like birdcages, aquariums should not be located where they will receive direct sunlight. Fish tanks are both heavy and fragile; they must be securely fastened so that there's no danger of tipping them over. Finally, a few phone calls will turn up people who are knowledgeable about fish and who are willing to help you with the specifics of fish selection and care.

15

Plants

A sterile environment compounds the unease that many families and friends feel about visiting a nursing home. Most would be glad to bring in an extra plant and otherwise get involved in Edenizing.

As you know by now, the Eden Alternative is dedicated to providing a context for life that is rich in biological diversity. An important building block is our large number of indoor plants. Robert Frost said, "What is green is gold." Fortunately, the many plant species that are suited to the typical nursing home environment are inexpensive and relatively easy to maintain.

Earlier I noted that *care* means helping another to grow. We've read of "horticulture therapy" programs that do much to introduce the mechanics of plant care into the schedule of nursing home activities. This is laudable. Even better, however, is to connect, in as many ways as possible, these mechanical activities with the act of giving care.

In addition to the benefits to the human spirit, we have reason to believe that the extensive use of plants in the nursing home can produce a real improvement in indoor air quality. Many buildings—particularly newer, energy-efficient ones—have problems with indoor air pollution, or the "sick building syndrome" that has drawn so much press coverage. The sources of such pollution include fumes from pressboard furniture, synthetic carpeting, cleaning products, and paint. According to Bill Wolverton, former head of environmental science at NASA, "nature has built into plants the ability to use our wastes for their nourishment.... [I]t's about time we humbled ourselves and used this system."[5]

While the exchange of carbon dioxide and oxygen by plants is well understood, research on the impact of plants on indoor quality is a recent development. Wolverton has confirmed through numerous experiments that some plants absorb harmful organic compounds from the atmosphere. As a result, he recommends several species as "all-around poison eaters." These include peace lily (*Spathiphyllum*), king of hearts (*Homalomena*), lady Jane (*Anthurium andraeanum*), and weeping fig (*Ficus benjamina*). Each of these plants removes substantial amounts of ambient ammonia, formaldehyde, and xylene. Peace lily also absorbs a great deal of the benzene released by paints and cleaning supplies. A good way to launch your own natural, indoor air conditioner is to place two or three plants per hundred square feet of living space in your nursing home.

Some plants are particularly known for their fragrance. Coupled with the toxin absorption mentioned above, this can make a room smell inviting and help reduce unpleasant odors.

Plants increase the relative humidity and decrease the number of bacteria in the air. From the onset of the Eden Alternative, we've found a striking decrease in the rate of urinary and respiratory tract infections at Chase (center-insert figure 8). There are surely many reasons for this decrease, but we wonder to what extent plants may have played a role.

---

[5]Bill Wolverton, "Plants and Soil Microorganisms: Removal of Formaldehyde, Xylene and Ammonia from the Indoor Environment," *Journal of the Mississippi Academy of Science*, August/September 1993.

We believe that it would be fascinating to replicate Wolverton's work on indoor air quality—performed mainly in private residences and office buildings—in the nursing home setting.

The First Step

The introduction and care of a large number and variety of plants does not have to be accomplished by "experts." Every community has people who can help a nursing home accomplish this goal. Begin by tapping the knowledge of residents, staff, and family members. Each of these groups has a vested interest in improving the quality of the nursing home environment.

Involving nurseries, florists, and garden centers is another way to include nursing home residents in the larger community. Stretch your budget by encouraging garden club members to volunteer their talents with plant care or horticultural crafts. Jointly sponsor events with garden centers and garden clubs. This will bring more people into the nursing home and will increase your chances of success. It's a win-win situation.

Plant Placement

The proper mix of floor plants and hanging plants depends largely on practical space requirements. The needs of residents and plants must be considered carefully.

At Chase, we designed "life poles" to increase the usable room space and to allow residents easy interaction with their birds and plants. The life pole is a movable, spring-loaded steel tube with flanges on the top and bottom that fit snugly between the floor and ceiling. Detachable hanging rods can be moved to whatever height and direction are deemed appropriate. (Note: Life poles are designed for concrete ceilings. For ceilings that will not support the tension, hooks can be strategically located in the suspended ceiling grid or drilled and screwed into drywall. Check with your maintenance staff and local hardware stores for suggestions.)

Plant Requirements

All plants have specific requirements for light, water, temperature, and nutrients in order to carry on photosynthesis and other life functions successfully.

Light

There are three broad types of light intensity: direct, indirect bright, and low. While some species may survive in more than one type of light, most plants grow best in only one.

Plants placed in sunlight are said to be in a direct light environment. South-facing windows receive direct light for most of the day. Areas receiving indirect bright light include west, east, and north windows, as well as locations near south and west windows that are brightly illuminated but do not receive direct rays. Dimly lit areas like hallways are considered low light areas. Few species do well in them. (Be advised, the term "low light" does not mean no light at all.)

Many areas in nursing homes do not receive much natural light. However, these areas are usually adequately supplied with artificial light, though the actual intensity varies. Fluorescent bulbs are used more frequently than incandescent bulbs because they use less energy and provide adequate light for reading and office work. Since fluorescent light is cooler and more diffuse, it should be located close to a plant. To provide enough light for growth and flowering, two 40-watt fluorescent bulbs should be placed within twelve inches of plants. Using four tubes doubles the intensity and provides for even better flowering and growth.

Incandescent light is much brighter than fluorescent light and can be focused on a particular plant or area. At a distance of four feet, a 150-watt PAR-38 fixture provides adequate intensity for plant processes. "Grow lights" work well, too, and are easy to use.

For a good discussion of light intensity and duration and their relationship to photosynthesis, consult *House Plants* by John Brookes (listed in bibliography at the end of the book).

Water

Houseplants generally grow better in a humid environment because most houseplant species originate from temperate and tropical zones. Vigorous growth requires adequate water and increased humidity. You can increase humidity in the following ways:

PLANT GROUPINGS — Group plants together to form a "microclimate"; the air surrounding a group of plants is more humid than the air around a single plant.

WET TRAYS — Set plants above a tray of gravel, coarse sand, or perlite that is kept wet.

BUFFERED AIR FLOWS — Avoid locations where excessive air movements will cause rapid water loss, especially when placing plants directly above a forced hot air duct. The high temperature can be advantageous to some plants, but increased flow from the heating system drains moisture from plant surfaces through transpiration. In this situation, place a buffer—such as the tray mentioned above—between the plant and the heating duct.

HIGH HUMIDITY AREAS—Locate plants where the humidity is highest. If lighting is sufficient, bathrooms and kitchens often make good locations.

HUMIDIFIERS—Use room humidifiers near plants, or, as a last-ditch effort, install a supplemental humidifier in the facility's heating system.

Above all, keep plants adequately watered; with a regular water supply, methods of increasing humidity may not be necessary. Watering plants adequately means providing just the right amount, neither too little nor too much. Don't arbitrarily water every plant without first checking its soil. This will give you a feel for the various "microclimates" within a nursing home and will help determine how often particular plants and areas need to be watered. Once again, there are no hard rules for the frequency of watering. It depend on variables such as room temperature, humidity, light intensity, type of growing medium, and type of container used.

Because containers have a bearing on the frequency of watering, the specific planter can be chosen with time and labor savings in mind. For instance, plants in clay pots need to be watered more frequently than those in plastic pots because moisture escapes through the clay walls. While this characteristic may actually be desirable for some species that dry out between waterings, such as ivy, plastic pots are lighter and often more durable.

One type of plastic planter, called a "self-watering pot," is actually two pots in one. The upper half holds the soil and the plant, while the bottom holds a supply of water that the plant uses through capillary action. These planters need some attention, but they greatly reduce the amount of labor required for plant maintenance and thus the long-term cost.

For an informative discussion of different types of pots and their respective pros and cons, see Ruth Shaw Ernst's *The Movable Garden: How to Use Potted Plants Indoors and Out to Create a Care-Free Year-Round Garden* (listed in bibliography).

Many plants benefit from a daily misting, and, as with birds, this is an opportunity for residents to become involved in giving care. Use a standard spritzer bottle. It is best to use a new bottle if you do not know what solution(s) it may have contained. Many household cleaners are toxic to plants, and residue in the bottle may damage them.

Temperature

Since most popular houseplants originate in warmer climates, provide a temperature as close as possible to their natural environment, generally in the range of 60–70°F during the day. This should be no problem for most nursing homes, which often have even higher daytime temperatures.

Many flowering plants and evergreens actually prefer slightly lower temperatures, ranging from 50–60°F during the day. These plants are great for enlivening a cool area, such as a sunroom or an enclosed patio. Many evergreen species need to have even lower winter temperatures to achieve a time of dormancy.

These temperatures are ideal ranges, and most plants will tolerate slight differences some of the time. In their native environments, plants may often experience a five- to ten-degree drop from daytime temperatures. This should be emulated in the nursing home. Do, however, avoid temperature differences of more than fifteen to twenty degrees.

Growth Media and Nutritional Requirements

The material in which a plant grows is called a growth medium. Some plants can survive in different types of media, but each plant requires specific management to meet water and nutrient requirements. For instance, some plants grow in soil, some in water (hydroponics), and some in soil-less media. Other plants are parasitic, such as epiphytes. Don't just dig up dirt and pop a plant into it; use specific growing mixes.

As the name suggests, soil-based plant mix contains a percentage of soil, usually in the form of garden loam. Soil holds water well, unlike clay, which tends to compact and lose water.

Potting mixes that do not contain soil are generally good for retaining water and offer less chance of insect infestation. Soilless mixes need more frequent fertilizing than soil-based mixes, however.

Cornell University's Cooperative Extension Program has devised a general potting mix that consists of equal parts garden loam, coarse sand or horticultural vermiculite, and peat moss. This mix provides good drainage of excess water but also adequate water retention and aeration for proper root growth. You can make this mix yourself when garden soil is available, but you can also purchase similar sterilized mixes in bags that will be free of weeds, insects, and diseases.

A recommended all-purpose soilless mix from Cornell can be purchased under brand names such as Jiff-Mix, Pro-Mix, and Redi-Earth, or make the following recipe yourself.

Cornell Peat-lite Mix

Vermiculite no. 2 size (sold as Terralite)	4 quarts
Shredded sphagnum peat moss	4 quarts
Limestone (preferably dolomitic)	1 tbsp
Superphosphate (20%)	2 tsp
10-10-10 fertilizer	1 tsp

In addition to light and water, plants need nutrients. For continued vigor, most foliage plants should be fertilized with a balanced 20-20-20 fertilizer. (These numbers represent the ratio of nitrogen, potassium, and phosphorus.) Water-soluble fertilizers such as Miracle Grow should be applied about every four weeks during the growth period—generally from March through October. With the exception of a few flowering species such as crown-of-thorns and wax begonia, most plants need a winter rest. This means that they require less water and no fertilizer from mid-October through spring, when the first signs of new growth appear.

Ask your local cooperative extension office for suggestions or helpful publications.

Selecting Species

A sterile environment compounds the unease that many families and friends feel about visiting a nursing home. Most would be glad to bring in an extra plant and otherwise get involved in Edenizing. To increase the number of useful plants, suggest that families and friends bring hardy varieties of seasonal favorites that can be planted outdoors after their use inside. Examples are hardy mums, poinsettias, and Easter lilies. Another approach is to encourage families to purchase foliage plants; unlike potted flowers, these can enliven a room for several years rather than for only a few weeks.

As mentioned, it's worth selecting plant species that are well suited to the hot, dry air and varying amounts of light found in nursing home environments. Foliage plants grown primarily for their greenery are easier to care for than flowering plants. The latter usually need at least a half day of direct sunlight to flower, whereas foliage species vary widely in their need for light. This requirement should not discourage you from cultivating flowering plants or from purchasing seasonal ones. Rather, it's a good idea to begin with an emphasis on foliage plants. (For recommendations and growing requirements, see the end-of-book section Foliage Plants Recommended for Nursing Homes.)

Epiphytes

Epiphytes are another category of plants that deserve mention. Because most epiphytes are arboreal—meaning that they grow in the tops of trees—they have a unique root system that absorbs necessary nutrients and moisture from the air rather than from soil. Some popular houseplants commonly grown in soil often do not do well because they are actually epiphytes and do not grow in soil in their native habitats. Epiphytes include orchids, bromeliads, Easter and Christmas cactus, Resurrection fern, and rhipsalis.

For a great introduction to the art of growing "air plants," read *Plants That Grow on Air* by Jack Kramer. Kramer suggests experimenting with ferns and philodendrons. While not all varieties of these two species are true epiphytes, most grow like them. For example, ferns do not need soil around their roots to grow. *Asplenium bulbiferum,* a fern native to New Zealand and Australia, is particularly good for dry areas and thus an ideal candidate for nursing homes. Likewise, many philodendron species naturally vine their way up tropical tree trunks.[6]

Depending on the physical and cognitive abilities of your residents, growing epiphytes may hold the most opportuni-

---

[6]Jack Kramer, *Plants That Grow on Air* (New York: Simon & Schuster, 1975).

ty for actively involving residents with plants. Most epiphytes need daily misting.

Since epiphytes also do not need soil, they don't need to be grown in traditional pots. This freedom offers many opportunities to be creative. For instance, combine several epiphytic species together to create a living picture frame.

Toxic Plants

Because the Edenized environment is home to people and animals who could be harmed by the ingestion of toxic plant materials, take note of the following toxic species: oleander (*Nerium oleander*), dumb canes (species of *Dieffenbachia*), elephant's ear (species of *Alocasia, Colocasia,* and *Caladium*), poinsettia, and azalea.

Oleander, though prized for its beautiful flowers, should not be permitted in a nursing home. The juice of its stem and leaves is toxic and could cause serious injury if ingested. Poinsettias and azaleas, on the other hand, are often given in abundance as seasonal gifts. Since these are considered only mildly poisonous and are generally short-lived indoors, their use should not be totally excluded. However, it's a good idea to advise family and friends of confused residents to choose another type of plant. In addition, cats often like to chew on foliage, so keep toxic plants out of cats' reach.

Outdoor poisonous plants commonly cultivated include oleander, rhododendron, foxglove (*Digitalis*), Russian olive, castor bean, and rhubarb. Foxglove and oleander should not be allowed at all. With careful consideration given to the location of the other species mentioned, however, the chance of poisoning can be lessened. You can address further questions about poisonous plants to your county extension agent or poison control office.

16

The Garden

Remember that diversity is the key to success.
A garden should have room for leisurely strolls,
vegetable and fruit production, flower and
herb beds, and wildlife.

Properly designed and constructed, a nursing home garden provides outstanding social, spiritual, and dietary benefits. Residents may take an active role in starting and transplanting seedlings, or they may creatively use a garden's products. At the very least, they will enjoy the colors and scents and take pleasure in eating fresh, truly homegrown food. While hundreds of good references on garden design, installation, and maintenance are available, this chapter discusses the special opportunities and challenges posed by the nursing home garden.

A handful of people who live at Chase are capable of becoming active gardeners, but this isn't the only way for residents to benefit. We eat vegetables grown in the garden; our kitchen staff cooks with them, as well as with herbs and edible flowers in season. Many older people also grew up socializing over food at canning bees while shucking corn and snapping beans. The garden encourages these social interactions.

Our gardens also supply raw materials for crafts such as wreaths and potpourri. Residents enjoy drying and pressing flowers and herbs, making pinecone bird feeders, collecting mints for afternoon tea parties, and arranging flowers.

You don't have to be an expert horticulturist to create a solid, usable garden design. Most important are a clear understanding of the needs you want the garden to fill and a working knowledge of the key annuals, perennials, shrubs, and trees that can help you meet these needs. Remember that diversity is the key to success. A garden should have room for leisurely strolls, vegetable and fruit production, flower and herb beds, and wildlife.

Principles of Design

When considering the outdoor space that surrounds a nursing home, it's important to think in terms of a habitat. Since there are many species with which you could be sharing this space, try to see your surroundings not only through the eyes of residents but also from the perspective of animals and plants before you begin work.

Here, too, it's helpful to challenge the status quo. As Sara Stein, author of *Noah's Garden*, states, "We had thought to make a place spacious by clearing it. But remove a ground bird's cover or a butterfly's flower and you have erased its space." Stein continues:

> I am neither a romantic nor an altruist. I let grass grow for a grouse, preserve dry-stone walls for toads, leave logs rotting in the woods for centipedes. I do this less because it's the decent thing to do than because it's the necessary thing to do. Each kind of microbe, animal, and plant possesses some minute portion of the know-how that makes the earth work. The loss of a species deletes some portion of organic intelligence and leaves the land more stupid. Gardeners who clear a wild plot, as we did, can easily notice its diminishing IQ because immediately the land needs planting, feeding, watering, cultivating, and pest

156

control, whereas before it knew how to manage all these things itself.[7]

The good news here is that nature is forgiving. While we may not be able to reverse the advance of African deserts, the many "suburban holes" Stein notes in the American landscape can be patched if we treat them as unified backyard habitats. As she puts it, "we cannot rail against those who destroy the rainforest or threaten the spotted owl when we have made our own backyards uninhabitable."[8]

Patience and a willingness to take small steps can bring early success. The simple act of replacing a portion of a facility's lawn with flower and vegetable beds will entice many creatures to return. One Chase resident can recall a time when the land behind our nursing home was a marsh, thick with tall grass. She remembers playing there with her friends more than eighty years ago. Since our gardens have laid the path for biological diversity, some of the snakes and butterflies she so vividly recalls are making their return.

I'm not saying that lawns are intrinsically bad. They do have their uses. For me, however, seeing a nursing home with a dull carpet of green at its edges is a reminder of how ruthlessly conventional practice has eliminated all kinds of diversity from the daily lives of residents. The result, both inside and out, is often a sterile, mundane, and ailing environment that requires more financial and human resources to maintain than a truly enlivened natural habitat requires.

So what can we do? As Stein points out, "benign neglect would not be restorative. . . . We can, however, set aside a

---

[7]Sara Stein, "Ecology Begins at Home," *House Beautiful*, March 1993, 42–49.
[8]Ibid.

portion of our yards to plant, if not altogether naturally, then at least in a way that is not alien to the theoretical ecosystems we inhabit."[9]

Creating a Backyard Habitat

The following suggestions have been adapted from an article by Diane Heilenman entitled "Turn Your Backyard into a Wildlife Habitat."[10]

NATIVE PLANTS—Use native plants arranged in clumps and large groupings, or "green corridors." Aim for year-round effect or food. Large clumps attract wildlife because they provide cover and protection from predators.

WATER—Provide water, which is often the most limiting factor in an urban environment. Make it shallow, no more than a few inches, and provide a floating log, rock, or other avenue of escape.

DEAD TREES—Be untidy. Leave dead trees in place; they provide shelter for some species. They can be an important source of food for animals that eat insects, grubs, and the like. Dead limbs should be trimmed to eliminate the hazard of falling branches.

SHELTER—Provide shelter by creating piles of brush, rocks, or logs. A discarded Christmas tree will provide a year's worth of shelter for nesting birds.

WEEDS—Adopt a weed if you want to attract butterflies. They're drawn to nettles, milkweed, ironweed, oxeye daisies,

---

[9]Ibid.

[10]*Rochester (NY) Democrat and Chronicle*, 11 December 1993.

goldenrod, black-eyed Susans, and purple coneflower. Asters and Japanese honeysuckle also attract butterflies.

FLOWERS—To attract hummingbirds, plant red flowers, such as catchfly and cardinal flower. For nectar early in the season, plant a succession of azaleas and rhododendrons. A good sequence of blooming plants may include pinxter; rose; catalpa tree; and flame, smooth, red, and longleaf rhododendron. Also plant some trumpet vine for habitat and food.

FOOD TREES—Plant food trees. Good food trees and shrubs include all oaks, maples, beeches, buckeyes, pecans, walnuts and hackberries. Other good choices are wild cherry, wild plum, crab apple, gray dogwood, serviceberry, viburnums, blueberries, chokecherry, and holly, and vines such as grapes, trumpet vine, and bittersweet.

COVER TREES—Plant cover trees. Good cover trees include red cedar, white pine, and arborvitae. It's best to plant a diversity of species, as opposed to a single tree or grouping.

BIRDHOUSES AND FEEDERS—If you have an open backyard, put out several bluebird houses, spaced seventy feet apart. If you don't have a lot of space, you can put out bird feeders to attract songbirds of all descriptions. An excellent reference is *The Backyard Birdwatcher: The Classic Guide to Enjoying Wild Birds Outside Your Back Door* by George H. Harrison (New York: Simon and Schuster, 1988).

Building a backyard habitat takes time and money. Fortunately, the more time you have, the less money you need. Nursing homes have plenty of time. It's perfectly reasonable to put together a ten-year plan and watch your habitat slowly reach fruition.

Accessibility

For any garden, and especially for a nursing home garden, accessibility is crucial. Elderly residents cannot and should not have to climb over misplaced obstacles or reach into a flower or vegetable bed that's too wide. Enlist the help of a garden designer or extension agent, if needed, although the bulk of planning should be done by those living and working in this newly emerging habitat.

Many residents are compelled to move about in their surroundings by wheelchair, so every nursing home garden must make accommodations for these conveyances. The two most important issues here are the pathway surface and the dimension—height, width, and depth—of the garden beds.

In conventional gardening, the advantages of raised beds are becoming more apparent, especially when the gardeners are elderly. Whether you use structures to contain soil, or simply mound it at a level above the surrounding ground, raised beds allow you to create an environment well suited to the needs of both plant and gardener. While more accessible however, the mounded raised bed is generally too low and thus out of the reach of most residents who use wheelchairs.

There are many ways to raise garden beds. Use concrete blocks to build a "pit" filled with composted soil. Residents can wheel up to the bed and reach inside to garden. (Concrete blocks come in a variety of colors and textures; plant climbing vines near the block wall if you're concerned about appearance.) The blocks are relatively wide, which diminishes the amount of planting space, but residents can start seeds in the openings. Trailing annuals such as alyssum, nasturtium, and cucumbers are good choices for cascading down the front of the wall.

The same effect can be created with garden walls made of wood that use thinner planks to take up less of the reachable space. When choosing the material to retain your raised beds, keep in mind that pressure-treated wood contains copper, chromium, and arsenic. All are toxic. (Is treated lumber safe for use with food crops? For a frank discussion of this issue, read the January 1994 issue of *Organic Gardening* magazine. The editors cite scientific studies showing that treated lumber releases toxic chemicals into the soil.)

Another way to make gardening more accessible is to build a garden table that residents can wheel up to and under. This arrangement allows residents to work straight ahead and with both hands. The trick is to build the table high enough to be wheeled under, deep enough to contain at least six inches of soil, and low enough to be at a comfortable working height for a person in a wheelchair. Six inches is not much soil, so the choice of plants is limited. Your best bets include radishes, lettuce, and shallow-rooted annual flowers. Remember that the soil will dry out quickly, so locate these beds in a partially shaded area or near a water source that can be used frequently.

Pathways pose another consideration in designing a garden. All wheelchairs need a relatively hard, smooth surface. The most obvious and common path material is concrete—a fine material for this purpose but one that generally does not blend into a natural setting. Three ways to enhance it are: (a) by adding color or texture; (b) by adding small pebbles to the poured surface before it sets; and (c) by setting slate or flagstone into the path.

Another suitable option is the use of crushed aggregate screening that can be "glued" together by a substance sold as Stabilizer™, a natural desert plant material that binds small rock particles together. The aggregate is mixed dry with the stabilizer and then laid on top of a crushed stone base. The mixture is then watered and rolled. After the pathway cures, damage to the surface can be repaired by raking, spreading, and watering the area. We've used this material in our garden pathways with great success.

In designing your garden, be creative, and use what you have most readily available. Consult the Garden Supplies section and the Indoor and Outdoor Gardening Bibliography at the end of the book. Then sit down and make a list of your available resources, as well as your strengths and weaknesses as a community. Doing so will help you start out on the right foot and will set the course of your future habitat.

17

The Risks

---

*Risk is a part of life that cannot be
totally eliminated. These new risks must be
understood, analyzed, and minimized.*

I remember the outcry that met early attempts to free nursing home residents from the restraints that bound them to beds and chairs. Opponents charged that residents would surely fall and injure themselves if they were untied. These folks were, in one way, correct. A few people did fall and hurt themselves when released from restraints. The larger truth, however, tells another story. Hundreds of thousands of others who had been restrained unnecessarily now were benefiting enormously from greater freedom of movement and personal dignity. Today it's hard to find a nursing home professional who believes that we should return to the old ways.

The Eden Alternative presents many of the same challenges. After all, the surest way to ensure that a resident is never scratched by a dog is to keep dogs out of the building. The best way to guarantee that a resident will never catch a cold from a child is to keep visiting children at a distance. And so it goes. Yes, an Edenizing nursing home does create new risks for residents. Risk is a part of life that cannot be totally eliminated. These new risks must be understood, analyzed, and minimized. We have found that there are five categories of risk to consider when a nursing home Edenizes.

The Risk of Illness

When it comes to spreading disease in the nursing home, one animal has, far and away, the worst record. History shows that it has caused serious illness—even death—whenever it has been introduced. Fortunately, most nursing homes with this type of animal have programs in place that attempt to control its enormous disease-spreading potential. Some progress has been made.

This animal is *Homo sapiens*, the human being. Despite this drawback, no one suggests eliminating people from nursing homes. A home operated by robots could slash the risk of infection, but who would want to live there? Who would accept being cared for by machines?

The nursing home staff, because of the good they do, are well worth the risk of infection they create. It's the same with animals. The original Eden Alternative project has been operating for five years now, and there is no record of a resident being infected by a bird, cat, dog, or rabbit.

The Risk of Injury

Here again, the animal most likely to injure a nursing home resident is a human being. We all recognize this potential, and nursing homes see the importance of screening applicants for staff positions. The applicant's background is investigated, references are checked, and an interview is conducted. After they are hired, new employees undergo training in residents' rights, facility safety routines, and standard policies and procedures. Finally, there is a probationary period.

This is exactly the way it should work with animals who live in a nursing home. Many animals—Bengal tiger cubs come to mind—are ill-suited to this environment and can pose a major danger to residents. Even among dogs and cats, there are potential problem areas. Many times I've been told of an adorable little puppy who was brought to live in a nursing home. Soon the puppy was chewing things up, jumping on people, and making a total nuisance of itself. Hands were thrown up, and the experiment was declared a failure. In my view, failure was preordained. After all, how many nursing homes recruit, train, and monitor their human staff members in such an irresponsible manner?

Preventing injuries to residents and staff by animals is a function of exactly the same principles that work to select, train, and retain a capable, safe human staff. Many groups have done work on the specific policies and procedures that are necessary to promote safe interaction among people, animals, and the environment. Foremost among them is the Delta Society. Making animals a safe part of the human habitat requires effort. Still, it is effort repaid with laughter and the twinkling of a resident's eye.

The Risk of Allergies

I learned an important lesson about allergies early in the initial Eden Alternative project. I was upstairs making medical rounds when the overhead speaker delivered a page for me on the first floor. This was unusual, and I raced down the stairwell to see what was wrong. When I arrived at the first-floor nurses' station, I saw a nurse sitting on a chair and gasping for air. Her skin had the blotchy red color of an allergic reaction. I called for an ambulance, and we grabbed the emergency drug box. I injected her with epinephrine and an antihistamine. Soon, the emergency squad arrived, and the nurse was taken to the nearest hospital.

When she was on her way, I remember thinking, "That's it, the Eden Alternative is finished. Surely her terrible allergic reaction is due to some part of the new habitat. If the Eden Alternative can cause an allergic reaction as bad as this, how can we continue?"

A week later, I was told that tests revealed an allergy to latex as the source of her problem. Latex is everywhere in a nursing home. It's in the gloves, medication vials, and supplies that are part of giving nursing care. Nurses use it every day.

Interestingly, no one suggested that we toss all the latex into the dumpster. Instead, we looked at how we could help this nurse avoid contact with it during her daily work. By applying a bit of ingenuity, we solved her problem, and she continues to perform her nursing duties without trouble.

What about the Eden Alternative, however? Can contact with plants and animals result in allergic reactions? Yes, it can, but this problem is more theoretical than practical. For starters, many nursing home residents who were troubled by allergies to animals as young adults no longer exhibit these allergies in later life. The body's immune system simply is not up to the task of creating an allergic reaction. The risk of allergies also depends on the amount of allergen present in the environment. A pet-owning apartment dweller with a relaxed attitude toward housekeeping must cope with a high level of animal dander in his or her home. In the nursing home, the number of animals per square foot is actually small, even with the large number that we have. The allergens are spread over a larger area and are therefore less likely to cause a problem. The nursing home is also cleaned effectively and regularly so that dander rarely accumulates. Finally, most nursing homes have efficient systems for moving air throughout the building, and this filtering tends to remove allergens.

When a problem does crop up, it can almost always be handled the way we handled the nurse's reaction. Some common sense and teamwork can alter the environment in ways that maintain the human habitat and minimize the risk of an allergic reaction.

The Risk of Legal Liability

Anyone in the United States can be sued at any time and for almost any reason. Except for the most neurotic among us, we accept that reality as part of the cost of living in a free society. The proper question is not Could I be sued? but rather Am I conducting myself in a manner consistent with my highest standards and most valued beliefs? In medical school, I learned that the best protection against a malpractice suit is to use all of your skill, training, knowledge, and experience to give your patient the best possible care. Hiding behind unnecessary tests and consultations serves to weaken rather than to strengthen your position.

Nursing homes can and should commit themselves to eliminating the plagues of loneliness, helplessness, and boredom. When they embrace the Eden Alternative, they accept the theoretical risk of a lawsuit in exchange for the enormous and ongoing benefits that the human habitat creates. It's that simple.

The Risk of Regulatory Sanction

Here at the Eden Alternative we have reviewed the public health laws of nearly all fifty states. They all share basic regulations prohibiting the introduction of animals into food service areas, but none have rules as restrictive as New York State's. This is ironic because New York State is where the Eden Alternative got its start.

The regulatory rule book exists to protect residents against those who would do less than they should to serve residents' needs. Nursing home inspectors are most interested in catching people who shirk their responsibilities either in the interest of profit or as a result of old-fashioned laziness. These inspectors have a much different attitude toward those who publicly commit themselves to enhancing residents' quality of life.

The first Eden Alternative is a case in point. The start-up costs for our project were underwritten by a grant from the New York State Department of Health. Meanwhile, the regional health department office granted us a waiver from the regulation that limited New York nursing homes to one dog or one cat and prohibited birds altogether. We rolled up our sleeves and went to work. Little did we know, but as we were filling our nursing home with plants, animals, and children, the state health department was belatedly discovering that the law did not permit a waiver in this area. We were stuck.

The date of our annual survey was coming up, and, boy, were we ever out of compliance. According to the rule book, we had 137 animals too many. Fortunately, the regional office had been keeping tabs on us, and they could see the impact the project was having on the quality of life the facility afforded to residents. They figured that if the surveyors didn't *notice* the animals (ones that had been purchased with Department of Health dollars), then we couldn't be penalized. I will always remember the sight of a surveyor grimly struggling not to notice Sanborne the cat as she sashayed across the pages of the chart he was reviewing.

The point is that the regulators could see and feel our passion for making the nursing home more natural and homelike. Our experience led to the passage of legislation that permits nursing homes in New York State freely to pursue all aspects of the Eden Alternative. Governor George Pataki signed the bill into law in the fall of 1995.

When it comes to dealing with regulators, I advise anxious administrators to be proactive. Normally, administrators are happiest when they see surveyors' backsides going out their door. They should change the rules of the game. Inviting the survey team in for a roundtable discussion of the Eden Alternative is a great way to start. The facility's own plans should be provided in advance of the meeting. The key is learning how to work with regulators so that they can be kept abreast of the Edenizing process. Rather than holding back, the proactive administrator solicits suggestions from regulators and asks for guidance in areas that may prove troublesome.

18

Other Places

*The principles of the Eden Alternative
can be applied anywhere people are troubled
by loneliness, helplessness, and boredom.*

Nursing homes are not the only places of human habitation in need of improvement. The principles of the Eden Alternative can be applied anywhere people are troubled by loneliness, helplessness, and boredom. You can Edenize your house or apartment or help someone you love Edenize theirs. The principles remain the same. There are, however, a few twists to keep in mind.

The Eden Alternative cannot be forced on people. As in the nursing home, the first step is education. Sit down with the person and talk about how animal companionship can take the sting out of loneliness. We find that many people who had neither the time for nor the interest in a pet in earlier years can gain great pleasure from an animal companion in later life.

Our friend Bob Keefe is a good case in point. Even in his mid-eighties, Bob worked part-time, drove his own car, and knew all the local waitresses by name. Still, he lived alone and often spoke of the loneliness he experienced in the evening. Some of his friends detected a problem and talked about getting him a parakeet. Bob let us know that he didn't really need a bird, but if we wanted to get him one it would probably be all right.

Bob immediately named his pale-blue pet "Billy," in my honor. He quickly learned how to take care of Billy, and

Billy took care of him. Sometimes at night our phone would ring, and Bob's happy voice would be on the other end: "You won't believe what that darned fool bird did tonight." Bob would let Billy out of the birdcage, and the bird would play fetch, chasing and retrieving a small plastic ball. When tired of the game, Billy would nestle quietly in Bob's lap for hours at a time.

A dog would have been more than Bob could have handled at that point in his life. The bird, however, was just right.

Bob's experience with Billy shows why, when Edenizing, it is important to be reasonable and practical. Some researchers have found that something as simple as the daily act of caring for a houseplant can have a positive impact on an individual's health and sense of well-being. However, it is equally important to remember that creating a situation where a person is not able to give adequate care to plants or animals can actually increase their feeling of helplessness.

Here are some general guidelines:

PLANTS—Plants require the least care and carry the smallest risk. They can be positioned close to the person, and simple plant-care equipment can be adapted for people who are physically disabled. Plants can also be well-cared for even with just occasional visits. See chapter 15 for suggestions, and start with easy-care plants that are likely to do well.

BIRDS AND CATS—Birds and cats require a similar amount of care. It's generally best to avoid unusual breeds of both species. From the Eden Alternative point of view, the key is finding the best balance between the amount of companionship given and the amount of care required. As in the nursing home, animals should come from a reputable source and be carefully examined by a vet before moving in.

DOGS—Dogs require the most care and depend heavily on the memory and judgment of their owners. Many apartment complexes and retirement communities place onerous restrictions on dog ownership or prohibit it altogether. Still, a healthy, happy, affectionate dog can provide an enormous amount of comfort and companionship.

Remember, it is best to start simply and to go slowly with whatever elements you incorporate into your habitat. Build on early success and keep your plans flexible. Your Eden Alternative should pass our three simple tests:

Are the elements of the habitat close to the people they are intended to help?

I remember, when speaking at a national conference, that during the question-and-answer period a woman rose to tell of a nursing home administrator in Colorado who kept a horse on the property. I applauded the administrator's willingness to do something unusual and asked how the residents were given contact with the horse. Unfortunately, the residents of that home had very little to do with the horse or any other animal.

Is the contact continuing?

Intermittent programs, while interesting and even invigorating, do not provide the continuity upon which true companionship is based. Continuity is also important because the plants and animals involved must be taken care of regularly. One woman I know recalls going through a long bout of depression and chronic illness. She was in bed up to sixteen hours a day but still managed to get up and around so that her cat would not suffer from neglect. In retrospect, she credits those daily chores with her ultimate recovery.

Does the contact promote human growth?

The Eden Alternative deals directly with the human spirit. As a physician, I can sometimes trick the body into recovery by administering drugs and treatments. The spirit, however, cannot be deceived. In the past, many older people drew strength directly from the community that nurtured them as children and governed them as adults. The Eden Alternative can help them to reconnect with that world by creating an environment of mutual support and sustenance. It can be a source of strength for us all.

Wouldn't we all be better off if we Edenized not only our homes but also our schools, neighborhoods, hospitals, parks, and prisons? The Eden Alternative got its start in the cold, sterile halls of a nursing home, but the need for a livable human habitat is one that we all share. By stopping, looking, listening, and feeling, we can understand the lessons the frail and institutionalized elderly are teaching us. Human beings, like all animals, need to be suited to their habitat. While our world sometimes seems to move us further away from this ideal, an Edenized nursing home, with its compassion and courage, helps to move us back.

Afterword

Edenizing will be accomplished by people from all walks of life.

As of the mid-1990s, we have constructed a system of institutional care for our society that reflects some of the best that medical technology has to offer. Unfortunately, the system is marked dramatically by some of the most depersonalizing, unnatural features of early twentieth-century asylums and poorhouses. In the nursing home, we have the opportunity to mold an environment that is an entire world for those who live there. I tour facility after facility, and I find them as warm and appetizing as old TV dinners. I'm often stunned by the disparity between the administrator's chirpy enthusiasm and the harsh reality of life inside the building. Is this the best we can do?

We lack for neither ideas nor effort. The long-term care industry bristles with new programs and therapies and all are well intentioned. Likewise, all accept as a given the fundamental assumptions that underlie the conventional nursing home. Rather than confront the status quo, most reform proposals confine themselves to debate over a new activities program here or revision of an established policy there. Our times demand something more. The bricks and mortar can remain as we rebuild the social institutions that are our nursing homes from the foundation up.

All of this is much more easily said than done. Nursing homes are conservative, cautious institutions that sometimes seem able to stifle even the most modest reforms. Still, I think this battle can be won. No nursing home is impervious to persistent pressure applied by true leaders.

Edenizing will be accomplished by people from all walks of life.

- ✧ Some nursing home professionals will hear the message. They will see how the philosophy provides an answer to some of their most fatiguing challenges. They will work in their facilities and within their professional organizations to promote change.

- ✧ Family members will find in these ideas a ray of hope for those they love. They can organize themselves and place the Eden Alternative on the nursing home's agenda of urgent issues. Their persistence will keep it there until the human habitat is brought to fruition.

- ✧ Some for-profit operators will see that today's model for nursing home care is a relic of the past; they will embrace the Eden Alternative as a model for the future.

- ✧ State regulators are already opening a dialogue that can lead to partnership with nursing homes and an ongoing improvement in the lot of those who live in them.

Leadership by the States

Currently, good examples of this kind of leadership can be found in Missouri and Texas. In Missouri, a forward-thinking lieutenant governor and state division on aging have developed the TEAM project (Teaching the Eden Alternative in Missouri). Sixty-eight of the state's long-term care facilities have joined together with the state university, regulators, and elected officials to work for the Edenizing of all the state's nursing homes. Their effort is bearing fruit because it has unwavering support from the top. Persistence is their watchword.

Texas is blazing its own trail with a legislature-authorized Texas Eden Alternative Pilot Project. Texans have successfully built on the Missouri model and have made a special effort to incorporate Southwest Texas University, its students, and its faculty into the project.

As this book goes to the printer, Nebraska, Alabama, Florida, Kansas, and Oklahoma are all investigating the possibility of setting up their own statewide projects.

Nursing homes were not allowed to pursue the Eden Alternative in New York State until September 1995, when Governor Pataki signed the bill into law lifting that prohibition. Now, less than one year later, eight homes are actively Edenizing in New York State.

Leadership by Individuals

What if you don't have the good fortune of living in one of these forward-looking states? There are plenty of pioneers out there building their own Eden Alternatives. Although they are too numerous to mention individually, several early leaders do deserve mention. John Mauch of Peabody Manor in Manchester, Indiana, stunned me by inviting dozens of members of the staff of a cross-town facility to a day-long training session his institution had sponsored. His generosity speaks well for his character and that of the organization he leads. Miriam Stermer of Methodist Home in Charlotte, North Carolina, continues to dazzle us with her careful precision and attention to the needs of her staff and residents.

Remember, you don't need to run a nursing home in order to get in the game. Danny Siegel, who heads the Ziv Tzedaka Fund, has crisscrossed this country and Israel, teaching people in synagogues and youth centers about what a wonderful *mitzvah* the Eden Alternative can be. As head of the local Alzheimer chapter, Lois Abeles has worked tirelessly in South Florida to see that the Eden Alternative takes root there.

Family members all over the United States are taking the simple step of bringing the Eden Alternative to the attention of the nursing home management and sharing it with other family members. Nursing home residents are getting into the act as well. They are inviting people knowledgeable about the Eden Alternative to address their resident councils. With so much at stake and so many shoulders put to the wheel, nursing homes will change.

For our part, Judy and I continue to take pleasure from teaching others about these ideas. In 1995, the demand for our time substantially exceeded our ability to meet with all the groups who wanted to hear our message. In the spring of 1996, we trained the first group of thirty Eden Alternative Associates. These folks have the knowledge and skills to help with the process, and they have an energizing commitment to the work of changing every nursing home in the United States.

So many people have written to us asking if we know of Edenizing nursing homes in their area that we have assembled an Eden Alternative directory that can help match residents with Edenizing homes. Of course, we continue to chronicle the growth of this movement with our quarterly *Friends of the Eden Alternative Newsletter*. If you would like to be added to the mailing list or if you want to contact us for any reason, please write, call, or send an electronic message:

Eden Alternative
RD1 Box 31B4
Sherburne, NY 13460
(607) 674-5232
Fax: (607) 674-6723
E-mail: rumpelst@norwich.net

Every reader of this book is a potential agent of change. No matter what your background, you can meet with the leadership of a nursing home you care about and introduce them to the Eden Alternative.

The idea belongs to no one. The obligation to recognize, appreciate, and fulfill the most basic social needs of the most frail and elderly of our fellow human beings belongs to us all.

Epilogue

I served happily as physician and medical director for Chase Memorial Nursing Home from April 1991 till February 1995. I will always remember those years for their exhilarating mixture of growth and camaraderie. Still, even good things must come to an end. I left my position at Chase in large part because of my conviction that Eden had become deeply rooted in the home's culture and would continue to flourish after my departure. This has proven to be the case. Also, I needed to be able to spread the ideas of the Eden Alternative as far and wide as I could.

This book is a vital part of our plan to bring every nursing home in America into contact with the principles and practices of the Eden Alternative. Even though I no longer have an official affiliation with Chase Memorial, I have maintained the use of "we" and "our" throughout the description of Eden at Chase because it was truly a team effort and because the problems and triumphs encountered by Chase are common to nearly every Edenizing home. I will continue this work until, with the help of the readers of this book, we have successfully combined nature, hope, and nursing homes.

Pet Resources

Birds. A friendly reference book that will help you to choose your birds as well as to care for, house, and feed them is *The Complete Bird Owner's Handbook* by Gary A. Gallerstein, D.V.M. It is available at the address and phone below:

> Howell Book House
> Macmillan Publishing Company
> 201 West 103rd Street
> Indianapolis, IN 46290
> (800) 428-5331

For bird and aviary equipment such as cages and feeders, contact one of the following mail-order companies:

> China Prairie Company
> Ettersburg Star Route
> Garberville, CA 95542
> (707) 986-7281

> UPCO (United Pharmical Company)
> 3705 Pear Street
> St. Joseph, MO 64502
> (800) 254-8726

Delta Society. For Canine and Feline Temperament Profiles:

> Delta Society® Pet Partners Program®
> 289 Perimeter Road East
> Renton, WA 98055-1329
> (800) 869-6898 ext. 23
> Fax: (206) 235-1076

Dogs and Cats. Write or call or dial on the Internet for this extensive collection of books and videos on dogs and cats:

> Dog and Cat Book Catalog
> Direct Book Service
> P.O. Box 2778
> Wenatchee, WA 98807
> (800) 776-2665
> E-mail: dgctbook@cascade.cascade.net

Greyhounds. For information on obtaining a retired racer, contact one of the following three organizations. The first two are listed only with their toll-free numbers because the addresses that are appropriate for you depend on your location. Call to receive a referral or information with regard to greyhound placement in your own area:

> Greyhound Pets of America
> (800) 366-1472

> National Greyhound Adoption Network
> (800) 446-8637

> USA Defenders of Greyhounds
> P.O. Box 1256
> Carmel, IN 46032
> (317) 244-0113

Rabbits. Filled with great candid photographs, the *House Rabbit Handbook: How to Live with an Urban Rabbit* by Marinell Harriman provides myriad tips for creating a safe, healthy, and fun atmosphere for your pet rabbits. It includes advice on everything from supplies, cages, and toilet training to proper diet and nutrition. There is also a section on acclimating pet rabbits to cats, dogs, and people. Order from Drollery Press:

Drollery Press
1524 Benton Street
Alameda, CA 94501
(510) 521-4087
E-mail: hrsdp@aol.com

Veterinary Publications and Supplies. Guides to farming, gardening, and raising livestock are available by the hundreds, ranging in cost from 25–50¢ (many) to $25 or more, from the University of Missouri. Send or call for the catalog:

Extension Publications
University of Missouri
2800 Maguire Blvd.
Columbia, MO 65211
(800) 292-0969

A basic veterinary reference for poultry and other animals that covers nutrition, immunizations, diseases, and treatment is the *Merck Veterinary Manual*, published by Merck and Co., Inc. It is available from Merck at the address and phone below; it is also available from Omaha Vaccine Co., listed next.

Merck Publishing Co.
P.O. Box 2000 RY7-220
Rahway, NJ 07065
(800) 659-6598

For veterinary supplies, feed, books, and equipment for all types of livestock and poultry, send or call for a free catalog:

Omaha Vaccine Co.
3030 L Street
Omaha, NE 68107
(800) 367-4444

Foliage Plants Recommended for Nursing Homes

Asparagus Fern: Requires less humidity than true ferns. Trim to keep size and shape desired.
(*Asparagus setaceus*) IBL, M/D, 70–75°F

Grape Ivy: May be pruned to any height.
(*Cissus rhombifolia*) IBL/LL, M, 65–70°F

Heartleaf Philodendron: Climbs on trellis. Easy vine to grow. Fertilize to keep leaves a good size.
(*Philodendron oxycardium* or *scandens*) IBL/LL, M/D, 70–75°F

Lipstick Plant: Very nice hanging plant. Deep red blossoms give this plant its name. Ideal for sunny bathrooms.
(*Aeschynanthus lobbianus* or *radicans*) DL, M, 60–70°F

Piggyback Plant: Adaptable. Water well when surface soil dries.
(*Tolmiea menziesii*) IBL, M, 45–50°F

Spade-leaf Philodendron: A great houseplant. Wash leaves each month with mild soap and water. Don't overwater.
(*Philodendron domesticum*) IBL, M, 70–75°F

DL = direct light, **IBL** = indirect bright light, **LL** = low light
M = moist, **D** = dry, **M/D** = soak thoroughly, then let dry

Spider Plant: Small flowers open in runners just before new plantlets form. Watering: water, and then when nearly dry, water again.
(*Chlorophytum elatum* or *comosum*) IBL, M, 50–55°F

Swedish Ivy: Rampant grower. Very tolerant.
(*Plectranthus australis* or *labiatae*) IBL, M, 50–70°F

Wandering Jew: Easy to grow. Propagate with 4- to 6-inch tip cuttings in water.
(*Tradescantia albiflora*) IBL, M/D, 50–60°F

Table and Windowsill Plants

Burro's Tail: Nice hanging succulent. Let it dry out between waterings; mist once per week.
(*Sedum morganianum*) DL, M/D, 50–70°F

Cast-Iron Plant: In the South this plant flourishes in dense shade.
(*Aspidistra elatior*) LL, M, 70–75°F

Chinese Evergreen: Guaranteed foolproof.
(*Aglaonema modestum*) LL, M, 70–75°F

Prayer Plant: Needs good humidity and moist soil; will tend to get brown otherwise. Every fall, trim off oldest or straggly leaves.
(*Maranta leuconeura*) IBL, M, 65–70°F

Snake Plant: Grows almost anywhere. Will flower if properly cared for.
(*Sansevieria trifasciata*) LL, M/D, 62–65°F

Floor Plants

Corn Plant: Several varieties. Excellent houseplant. When becomes leggy, air-layer and repot.
(*Dracaena* species) IBL/LL, M, 70–75°F

Norfolk Island Pine: Keep potbound to limit size. Keep cool with lots of light. Lower needles turn brown if allowed to overdry.
(*Araucaria heterophylla*) DL, M, 50–55°F

Palms: Very tolerant of dim light, but need warmth. Never let soil ball dry out.
(*Palmaceae* species) LL, M, 65–70°F

Peace Lily: Does well in most any location outside of direct light. White, hoodlike flowers and large, deep-green foliage. Good at filtering many types of indoor air pollutants.
(*Spathiphyllum* species) IBL/LL, M, 70–75°F

Podocarpus: A coniferous evergreen that remains conveniently small. Useful for bonsai. Best at a cooler temperature.
(*Podocarpus nagi*) DL, M, 60–65°F

India Rubber Plant: Rugged houseplant. Leaves apt to drop if plant is chilled or if moved from one place to another.
(*Ficus elastica*) IBL/DL, M, 65–75°F

Umbrella Tree: Good apartment plant. To keep within bounds, cut the main trunk and let it remain a potbound cluster plant. Watering: soak, allow to dry completely, then soak again.
(*Brassaia actinophylla* or *Schefflera*) IBL, M, 70–75°F

DL = direct light, **IBL** = indirect bright light, **LL** = low light
M = moist, **D** = dry, **M/D** = soak thoroughly, then let dry

---

Garden Supplies

The Cook's Garden   **(802) 824-3400**
P.O. Box 535, Londonderry, VT 05148
   Vegetable and flower seeds; especially large selection of salad greens; catalog free.

Johnny's Select Seeds   **(207) 437-4357**
310 Foss Hill Rd., Albion, ME 04910
   Vegetable, herb, flower, and specialty seeds; detailed culturing information in catalog; catalog free.

Logees Greenhouse   **(860) 774-8038**
141 North Street, Danielson, CT 06239
   Wide selection of rare house plants, including succulents and epiphytes; catalog $3, refundable with first order.

Michigan Bulb Co.   **(616) 771-9500**
1950 Waldorf NW, Grand Rapids, MI 49550
   Low-cost source for bulbs and perennials; cut-rate prices on mixed bulbs for naturalizing; catalog free.

Missouri Dept. of Conservation   **(573) 751-4115**
P.O. Box 180, Jefferson City, MO 65102
   Every autumn, the department offers the "backyard wildlife bundle" of tree seedlings, shrubs, and perennial wildflowers for next to nothing. These are shipped in February, but supplies are limited, so order early. The department also sells a variety of trees (usually bare rootstock, 2–3 years old), such as pines, redbud, silver dogwood, pinoaks, and tulip poplar. Write for an order form.

Seeds of Change　　　　　　　　**(505) 438-8080**
P.O. Box 15700, Santa Fe, NM 87506

More than 500 varieties of certified organic seeds; open-pollinated food plants, herbs, and flowers; traditional heirloom varieties a specialty; catalog free.

Seed Savers Exchange　　　　　　**(319) 382-5990**
3076 North Winn Rd., Decorah, IA 52101

A grass-roots coalition of backyard gardeners who, through membership, have access to and help preserve thousands of heirloom vegetable, fruit, and nut varieties; membership $25 U.S., $30 Canada; brochure $1.

Southern Exposure Seed Exchange　　**(804) 973-4703**
P.O. Box 170, Earlysville, VA 22936

Open-pollinated, disease-resistant vegetable varieties; many heirlooms; multiplier onions, garlic, herbs, sunflowers, and uncommon vegetables. Send SASE for price list; catalog and garden guide $2, refundable with first order.

Stokes Seeds, Inc.　　　　　　　**(716) 695-6980**
P.O. Box 548, Buffalo, NY 14240

More than 2500 varieties of vegetable and flower seeds; catalog contains detailed growing information; catalog free.

W. Atlee Burpee and Co.　　　　　**(800) 888-1447**
300 Park Ave., Warminster, PA 18974

Large selection of flowers, vegetables, fruit, and nursery stock; catalog can be used as a reference; catalog free.

Worm's Way　　　　　　　　　**(812) 876-6425**
7850 North Highway 37, Bloomington, IN 47404

Catalog features wide array of hydroponic equipment and helpful information to get you started; catalog free.

Indoor and Outdoor Gardening Bibliography

Hooked on the Internet? You may want to visit the site of the National Wildlife Federation's Backyard Wildlife Habitat Program. That address is—

http://www.nwf.org/nwf/prog/habitats

Horticultural Therapists. These are professionals who have developed the unique skills required to facilitate successful interactions between people and plants. They know how to employ methods for making the gardening experience accessible to all, and they understand how to integrate the garden's many harvests into meaningful activities. You may want to contact this organization for information:

American Horticultural Therapy Association (AHTA)
362A Christopher Avenue
Gaithersburg, MD 20879
(800) 634-1603
E-mail: 75352.122@compuserve.com

Good Books. Following are some good resources available at libraries and bookstores or directly from the publishers.

Adil, Janeen R. *Accessible Gardening for People with Physical Disabilities: A Guide to Methods, Tools, and Plants.* Rockville, MD: Woodbine House, 1994.
    This book makes it possible for individuals to garden even if they use a walker, if they are in a wheelchair, or if

they have limited upper body strength. Learn how to create a garden using raised beds, containers, or vertical gardens with the help of easy-to-follow instructions, drawings, and photographs.

Bartholomew, Mel. *Square Foot Gardening.* Emmaus, PA: Rodale Press, 1981.

This is a well-written, easy-to-follow manual on intensive gardening. Raised beds can be designed right into the landscape, and the square foot method makes it easy for staff, residents, and children to stake their claim and get growing.

Bradley, Fern Marshall, and Ellis, Barbara W., eds. *Rodale's All-New Encyclopedia of Organic Gardening: The Indispensable Resource for Every Gardener.* Emmaus, PA: Rodale Press, 1992.

A revered reference on all facets of gardening, this is the one gardening book that an Edenizing nursing home shouldn't be without.

Brookes, John, contributing ed. *House Plants.* Pleasantville, NY: The Readers Digest Association, Inc., 1990.

Add some style to your Edenizing! Presented in full-color, this book not only tells how to choose and care for your plants but also shows how to arrange them in new and exciting ways.

Brookes, John. *The Indoor Garden Book.* New York: Crown Publishers, 1986.

This is a good overview of how plants and plant products can be used to decorate the interior landscape. When you decide to make an institution more like a home, this book is a great source of ideas.

Constable, George [editor]. *Flowering Houseplants.* Alexandria, VA: Time-Life Books, Inc., 1990.

While flowering plants are generally more difficult to care for than most foliage plants, this book offers good advice on their special needs.

Ernst, Ruth Shaw. *The Movable Garden: How to Use Potted Plants Indoors and Out to Create a Care-Free Year-Round Garden.* Chester, CT: The Globe Pequot Press, 1991.

As the author suggests, growing plants in pots is a way to extend the gardening season once winter sets in. If you decide to begin Edenizing with plants inside your home, then this is also a good reference for the next logical step—expanding your garden to the outdoors, using containers. From there you might want to move on to raised flower and vegetable beds.

Fischer, Charles C., and Fox, Raymond T. *The Selection, Care, and Use of Plants in the Home.* Ithaca, NY: Cornell University Cooperative Extension, 1984.

In this succinct primer on houseplant care, recommended plant species are organized according to light requirements. Once you have gained experience with foliage plants, this is a good source of information on growing flowering plants.

Hallowell, Christopher. "Clearing the Air." *House Beautiful,* March, 1993, pp. 52–56.

This article describes Bill Wolverton's extensive research on how some houseplants can improve indoor air quality.

Halpin, Anne M. *Rodale's Encyclopedia of Indoor Gardening.* Emmaus, PA: Rodale Press, 1980.

For those particularly concerned with caring for houseplants in a manner safe not only for plants but also for pets and residents, this thorough reference covers species from foliage plants to vegetables and herbs, from bonsai to carnivorous plants, from trees and shrubs to aquatic plants.

Hayward, Gordon. *Garden Paths: Inspiring Designs and Practical Projects.* Charlotte, VT: Camden House Publishing, 1993.

This inspiring and beautifully illustrated book suggests many alternatives to the standard concrete sidewalk.

Jordan, William H. *Windowsill Ecology.* Emmaus, PA: Rodale Press, 1977.

In keeping with the idea of creating vibrant, diversified indoor habitats, this book is a great resource on using beneficial insects to control indoor plant pests. Before you run out and buy poisonous "housekeeping" products, pick up this book.

Kirkpatrick, Debra. *Using Herbs in the Landscape: How to Design and Grow Gardens of Herbal Annuals, Perennials, Shrubs, & Trees.* Harrisburg, PA: Stackpole Books, 1992.

The use of herbs in garden designs is a potential waiting to be explored. Herbs can animate a scene and stimulate the senses with their beauty and aromatic qualities. Herbal plantings are appropriate anywhere people congregate, meditate, pause, or pass by.

Kramer, Jack. *A Seasonal Guide to Indoor Gardening.* New York: Lyons & Burford, 1992.

This is a complete handbook to the changing needs of over 200 different houseplants throughout the year, with specific notes on what to do in spring, summer, winter, and fall. An extensive section in each seasonal segment of the book covers houseplants that are at their best in each season.

Kramer, Jack. *Plants That Grow on Air.* New York: Simon and Schuster, 1975.

A good book for intergenerational experimenting, this is about epiphytes: plants that obtain most if not all moisture and nutrients through the air rather than the soil. Many of the plants described here are well suited for nursing home environments.

Lamancusa, Kathy. *Guide to Wreath Making.* Blue Ridge Summit, PA: Tab Books, 1991.

A plethora of ideas are presented for using your garden produce to decorate your home.

Loewer, H. Peter. *The Indoor Window Garden: A Guide to More Than 50 Beautiful and Unusual Plants That Will Flourish Year-Round in Your Home.* Chicago: Contemporary Books, 1990.

Here is a practical guide with helpful hints for growing about fifty different kinds of indoor plants. The book includes a section on ornamental grasses suited for growing indoors.

Loewer, H. Peter. *The Indoor Water Gardener's How-To Handbook.* New York: Popular Library, 1976.

This is a wonderfully concise book, illustrating methods not only for starting houseplants in water, but for actually *growing* many species in water. Hydroponics is another good intergenerational activity.

Marcin, Marietta Marshall. *The Herbal Tea Garden: Planning, Planting, Harvesting & Brewing.* Pownal, VT: Storey Communications Inc., 1993.

Everything you need to re-create the tea tradition is in this book.

Oster, Maggie. *Gifts and Crafts from the Garden: Over 100 Easy-to-Make Projects.* New York: Wings Books, 1993.

This is a good resource for crafters and includes teas, potpourris, wreaths, dried flowers, and other gifts.

Ottesen, Carol. *Ornamental Grasses: The Amber Wave.* New York: McGraw Publishing Co., 1995.

Grasses provide cover and beauty in the garden.

Perper, Hazel. *The Indoor How-To Book of Oats, Peas, Beans, and Other Pretty Plants.* New York: The Viking Press, Inc., 1975.

This is an older but good work that introduces the idea of using common vegetables and grains as interesting, decorative, and educational plants indoors. This, too, is a great intergenerational experiment.

Phillips, Ellen, and Burrell, Colston C. *Rodale's Illustrated Encyclopedia of Perennials.* Emmaus, PA: Rodale Press, 1993.

In this wonderfully illustrated guide to the propagation and care of many popular perennials, photographs offer a preview of what your plants will look like before you dig in.

Rapp, Joel. *Mr. Mother Earth's Most Rewarding Houseplants.* New York: Fawcett Columbine, 1989.

Have fun with this light-spirited guide to plants that are worth trying. Not all of the recommended species are easy to grow, especially in arid environments. The author lists light, temperature, and humidity requirements for recommended species.

Relf, Diane. "The Accessible Garden." *Flower and Garden* December/January, 1994, pp. 40–42.

For planning accessibility, this article is a must.

Rothert, Gene. *The Enabling Garden.* Dallas: Taylor Publishing Co., 1994.

In a profession described at the beginning of this bibliography, the author is a Registered Horticultural Therapist (H.T.R.).

Stein, Sara Bonnett. *Noah's Garden: Restoring the Ecology of Our Own Back Yards.* Boston: Houghton Mifflin Co., 1995.

Here is both a delightful and challenging reflection on the dominant world view of gardeners. Stein argues that the responsibility of sound ecological practices must begin in the back yards of homeowners and not be focused on rain-forests around the globe. This is easy reading and an enjoyable guide for creating outdoor space that balances the needs of nature and gardeners. A portion of this work is excerpted in the March 1993 issue of *House Beautiful.*

Storey/Garden Way Publishing Bulletin Series. Pownal, VT: Storey Communications, Inc.

Storey Communications puts out well over one hundred of these 20- to 40-page guides on "country wisdom." The great thing is that you don't have to live in the country to take advantage of these informative booklets. Topics range from planting wildflower meadows to raising rabbits, from planning and planting a dwarf fruit orchard to making candy, and from starting seeds indoors to growing fifteen herbs for the kitchen. Publications cost less than two dollars each. These are highly recommended.

"Treated Wood: Yes It's Still Toxic!" *Organic Gardening.* January 1994, pp. 71–74.

In this scathing article in response to the claim that "treated wood is safe," the editors of the magazine offer to send a list of studies showing the dangers. Take the time to investigate and make an informed decision.

Whitner, Jan Kowalczewski. *Stonescaping: A Guide to Using Stone in Your Garden.* Pownal, VT: Garden Way Publishing, 1992.

A very good guide to the use of stone for walks, walls, and accents in your garden.

Yeomans, Kathleen, R.N. *The Able Gardener: Overcoming Barriers of Age and Physical Limitations.* Pownal, VT: Garden Way Publishing, 1993.

This book is another favorite of horticultural therapists.

Acknowledgments

From the beginning, the Eden Alternative has been a collaborative effort. It never would have been possible without the support and guidance of the people who live in, work in, and care about Chase Memorial Nursing Home.

I am deeply indebted to the residents of Chase for their patience and understanding as we fumbled our way through the early days. I have special appreciation for Mildred Angell and Margaret Bartlett, who have provided continual, articulate support for the Eden Alternative.

The Chase management team deserves recognition for its wonderful flexibility. Roger Halbert, Lois Griesing, Debbie Grainger, Laura Wilcox, Telford Rowe, Heather Anderson, Grace Lloyd, Sheila Frink, Connie Austin, Heather Morgan, Sue Holbert, Joyce Costine, and Mike Barbetta always put the residents' needs first. If I could, I would name every Chase employee and volunteer because they all nurtured our human habitat.

Special thanks are due to those who gave us the technical guidance we needed to make our project a success. Nick and Linda Esposito brought clarity and rigor to an evaluation plan that was, originally, as clear as mud. My wife, Judy Meyers Thomas, served with distinction as one of the original "Edenites" and contributed enormously to our understanding of animal care in the nursing home. Dave Betler deserves credit for his work on the "greening" of our nursing home inside and out. I benefited greatly from his experience and research. Veet Deha showed us the value of expert garden design. Paula Britten, Marsha Honsaker, Mike Virgil, and our child-care staff all deserve credit for breaking new ground in bridging the generations.

The New York State Department of Health funded our preliminary work, and we were helped especially by Dr. Mary Jane Koren and Liz Pohlman. Norm Andrzejewski deserves credit as our guardian angel.

Roger Wilson, Lieutenant Governor of Missouri, and the state's progressive Division of Aging deserve rich praise for preparing the ground for Edenizing Missouri's nursing homes and, ultimately, for improving the quality of life for all those who will learn from Missouri's leadership in long-term care.

Index

*A*beles, Lois, 177
Accessibility, in garden, 160–162
Accountability, 77, 79
Actions, chart of, to promote the
    Eden Alternative, 94
Administrators
  as leaders, 61–70
  as naysayers, 65, 66, 93, 95
  as promoters of change, 94
After-school program. *See* Child care
Aide. *See* Certified nurse aide
Air plants, 152
Air quality, 143–145
Allergen, 166–167
Allergy, risk of, 165–167
Anchor person, team's need for, 78
Animal Diet Policy, 119
Animals. *See also* Birds; Cats;
    Chickens; Dogs; Fish; Rabbits
  as creators of happenings, 39
  essential features of, for nursing
    home, 139
  and risk of allergies, 165–167
  and risk of injury to residents, 165
Antidepressants, 52. *See also* Drugs
Aquarium, 141–142
Artificial light, effect on plants,
    146–147
Asylums: Essays on the Social Situation
    of Mental Patients and Other
    Inmates (Goffman), 11
Attention, desire for, 47–48
Aviary, 130–131

*B*ackyard Birdwatcher: The Classic
    Guide to Enjoying Wild Birds
    Outside Your Back Door
    (Harrison), 159
Backyard habitat, 158–159

Backyard Wildlife Habitat Program,
  189
Bacteria in air, 144
Beck, Alan *(Between Pets and People:*
    The Importance of Animal
    Companionship), 59n
Begonia, in study opposite parakeets,
  59
Benefits
  as an area to address when pro-
    moting Edenizing, 96
  of birds, 127–128
  of cats, 121
  of dogs, 111, 120
  of Eden Alternative, 1–2, 44–46,
    52–53
  of the garden, 155–156
  of plants, 143–145
  of summer camp, 104
Between Pets and People: The Impor-
    tance of Animal Companionship
    (Beck and Katcher), 59n
Biological diversity, 31–32, 157
Birdcages, 129–130
Birdhouses, 159
Birdmobile, 134–135
Birds, 35–37, 127–137. *See also indi-*
    vidual types of birds
  aviary for, 130–131
  benefits of, 127–128
  cages for, 129–130
  diet of, 133–134
  guidelines for, chart of, 136
  illness in, signs of, 132, 137
  misting, 133
  pairing, 132–133
  schedule for, chart of, 137
  when Edenizing outside the realm
    of a nursing home, 172–173

Boredom
  evidence of, in residents, 48
  as a plague, 23–25
Butterflies, garden plants that
    attract, 158–159

Canaries, 131–132
Canine Temperament Profile, 114,
    117
Care
  human need for opportunity to,
    28–29
  principles of, 22–23
  versus treatment, 1, 8–15, 19–25,
    47–49
Cat pole, 38–39
Cats, 38–39, 121–126
  benefits of, 121
  diet, or food for, 123–124
  and litter boxes, 124–126
  number to have, 122–123
  and risk, 126
  selection criteria for, 121–122
  steps to success with, 122–124
  when Edenizing outside the
    realm of a nursing home,
    172–173
Certified nurse aide (CNA), 71–74
  definition of, 72
  and self-scheduling, 77–79
Change
  feeling threatened by, 67–68
  helping to promote, 90–98
  ingredients of successful, 64–65
  as a requirement of excellence,
    62–63
Chase Memorial Nursing Home
  compared with control facility,
    50–52, 56–57, 75
  location of, 2
  schedules and policies of, 108,
    109–110, 116, 119, 125, 136,
    137
  at start of changes, 27–28
Chickens, 140–141
"Chicken tractor," 141

Child care. *See also* Costs; Exchange
    students; Volunteers
  after school and on holidays,
    102–103
  on-site, 42, 102
  and regulations, 102
  societal need for, 99–102
  at summer camp, 104
  on vacation days, 103–104
Children, 30, 41–43, 99–110
CNA. *See* Certified nurse aide
Cockatiels, 129
Communities, human, 32
Community groups, hosting of, at
    nursing home, 106
Community involvement, with
    plants, 145
Companionship
  with birds, 132
  human need for, 28
  as treatment for loneliness, 24
Compositions, by student volun-
    teers, 105–106
Control facility
  compared with Chase, 50–52,
    56–57, 75
  description of, 50
Cornell Peat-lite Mix, recipe for, 150
Cornell University's Cooperative
    Extension Program, 150
Costs
  of after-school and camp pro-
    grams, 42, 103
  as an area to address when pro-
    moting Edenizing, 96
  of aviary, 130–131
  of nurse aide position, 75
  per prescription, 50
  of providing care, 14
  per resident for prescription drugs,
    20
  for startup of child-care center, 102
  of summer camp, 104
  "swinging" among centers of, 128
  trend line of health-care, 51
  versus value, 14

Cover trees, 159
Crate, for dog, 115
Cross-training (of staff members), 80
Curiosity, as a means to uncover and confront problems, 62

*D*ay care. *See* Child care
Death, 55–59. *See also* Mortality rate
Death certificate, 55, 56
Declawing cats, 123
Delta Society, 114, 117, 122, 165
Desipramine, 24. *See also* Drugs
Diabetes, contrasted with loneliness, 25
Diet. *See also* Birds; Cats; Dogs
    policy for animals, 119
    of residents, 20
Diversity
    benefits of, 84
    biological, 31–32, 157
    harmonized, 33
    social, 32–33
Dogs, 111–120
    benefits of, 111, 120
    comprehensive "care plan" for, 118
    diet of, 118–119
    equipment for, 114–115
    and fallen resident, 120
    greyhounds, 113
    health of, 117–118
    introducing into nursing home, 114
    number to have, 112
    persons responsible for, 37–38, 112
    rations for, to avoid obesity, 118–119
    as resident's personal pet, 113
    risks in having, 119–120
    schedule for, 116
    veterinary guidelines for, 115–118
    when Edenizing outside the realm of a nursing home, 173

Drugs
    alternatives to psychotropic, 52
    antidepressants, 52
    comparison of use at Chase before and after Edenizing, 52
    versus control facility, 50–51
    versus national data, 52
    decline in mind- and mood-altering, 51
    desipramine, 24
    haloperidol, 23, 52
    number of prescriptions per resident, 50
    overprescription of, 47–49
    reduction in use of, 47–53

*E*den Activities people, 43, 75, 128
Eden Alternative
    benefits of, 1–2, 44–46, 52–53
    directory of homes adopting the, 178
    the first, 35–46
    how to contact, 178–179
    as a new way of thinking, 2
    principles of formation of, 32–33
    ten principles of, 66
Eden Alternative Associates, 178
Eden Alternative Effect, 46, 51
Eden Alternative School, 107
Eden Alternative Vision, 91
Edenizing
    areas to address when promoting, 96
    outside the realm of a nursing home, 171–174
    people who will accomplish, 176
    and transforming of physical versus social environment, 68–70
Eden Principles, as true in an Edenizing nursing home, 65, 66
Egg mix for birds, 133
Empowerment
    of employees, 71–86
    of residents, 92

Epiphytes, 152–153
Ernst, Ruth Shaw *(The Movable Garden: How to Use Potted Plants Indoors and Out to Create a Care-Free Year-Round Garden),* 149
Evolutionary process, Edenizing as an, 40
Evolution of management styles at Chase, diagrams of, 82–83
Exchange students, 104–106, 108

*F*able (Kahlid the Kind), 17–18
Family members and residents as promoters of change, 94
Family structure and roles played, 99–101
Feeders, 159
Feline Temperament Profile, 122, 123
Fertilizer, 151
Financing. *See* Costs; Grant funding
Finches, 131
Fish, 141–142
Fleas, 118, 123
Flowering plants, 151–152
Fluorescent light, effect on plants, 146–147
Foliage plants, 151–152
Food supplements for birds, 134
Food trees, 159
Fox, Michael *(Understand Your Pet: Pet Care and Humane Concerns),* 128–129, 129n
Friends of the Eden Alternative Newsletter, 178
Frost, Robert, 143
Funding. *See* Costs; Grant funding

*G*arden, the, 40–41, 155–162
accessibility in, 160–162
as a backyard habitat, 158–159
benefits of, 155–156
design of, 156–162
flowers in, 159
pathways in, 161–162
with raised beds, 160–162
trees in, 159
weeds in, 158–159
Garden beds, raised, 160–161
Garden table, construction of, 161
Goffman, Erving *(Asylums: Essays on the Social Situation of Mental Patients and Other Inmates),* 11
Golden Rule of nursing home management, 70
Grant funding, 28, 102
Greyhounds, 113
Griesing, Lois, 75–86
Grit, for birds, 134
Grooming, of dog, 115
"Grow lights," 147
Growth, residents' capacity for, 22, 24
Growth medium, for plants, 149–150
Guidelines. *See* Policies; Schedules

*H*abitat,
human, start of, at Chase, 30–34
natural, 31–33
Haloperidol, 23, 52. *See also* Drugs
Harmony and harmonized diversity, 33
Harrison, George *(The Backyard Birdwatcher: The Classic Guide to Enjoying Wild Birds Outside Your Back Door),* 159
Harvard Medical School, xi–xii
Heartworm, 117
Heilenman, Diane (article on backyard habitat), 158
Helplessness, as a plague, 23–25
Horticulture therapy, 143, 191
Housekeepers, as team members, 75
Houseplants. *See* Plants
Human habitat, start of, at Chase, 30–34
Humidifiers, for plants, 148
Humidity, and plants, 148
Hummingbirds, 159
Hydroponics, 150

*I*llness, risk of, 164
Incandescent light, effect on plants,
147
Infections, decrease in, 144
Injury, risk of, 164–165
Inspectors, 168–169
Institutions. *See* Total institutions
Interview, with Lois Griesing, 75–
86

*J*ob-sharing, by certified nurse
aides, 78–79
Journal entries, by staff, 36–37

*K*ahlid the Kind, 17–18, 22
Katcher, Aaron *(Between Pets and
People: The Importance of Animal
Companionship)*, 59n
Keefe, Bob, 171–172
Kramer, Jack *(Plants That Grow on
Air)*, 152

*L*atex, allergy to, 166
Leadership, 61–70
by administrators, 176
by individuals, 177–178
issues addressed by, in long-term
care, 61–63
by states, 176–177
Legal liability. *See* Risks
Life pole, 36, 145–146
Light intensity as a plant require-
ment, 146
Litter boxes, 124–126, 140
Loneliness
as a killer, 56
as a plague, 23–25
Long-term care facility versus nurs-
ing home, 8–9
Lovebirds, 129
Lumber, and food crops, 161
Lyme disease, 117

*M*anagement styles, 76, 82–83. *See
also* Leadership
Mauch, John, 177

Medicaid, 8
Medical model of care, and level of
medication use, 49, 53. *See also*
Care versus treatment
Medicare, 8
Medication. *See* Drugs
Medication cart, 135
Medication reduction, 47–53
Meetings, mandatory weekly, 67
Methodist Home, 177
Middle school
children, 43
exchange students, 104–106
Military management system, 69
Mineral attachments for birds, 134
Money. *See* Costs
Morale. *See also* Reason to live
improvement in Mr. L.'s, 45
improvement in Mrs. B.'s, 57–58
improvements in, due to
Edenizing or team building,
36–37, 68, 75, 81, 84
Mortality rate, 56–57
*Movable Garden: How to Use Potted
Plants Indoors and Out to Create a
Care-Free Year-Round Garden*
(Ernst), 149
Mugford, Rodger, 58

*N*ational Wildlife Federation, 191
Natural habitat, 31–33
Need, human
to care for others, 28–29
for companionship, 28
to continue caring for pets, 58
perceived versus real, for medications, 48–49
for a reason to live, 57, 59
of residents
as definers of help received, 22
as definers of appropriate diversity, 33
for variety, 29
Nesting box, 139
*Newsletter, Friends of the Eden
Alternative*, 178

New York State Department of
    Health, 28, 168
Noah's Garden (Stein), 156–158
Nurse aide. *See* Certified nurse aide
Nursing department, reorganizing
    of, during Edenizing, 74–75,
    76–86
Nursing homes, number of
    Edenizing, 2, 176
Nutrients, for plants, 151
Nutrition. *See* Diet

*O*bjections, 93, 95, 163–169
    to dogs, 111
    to Edenizing, 65, 67–68
    by nursing middle management,
        74–75
    practical versus fearful, 67
Obligation, weakening sense of, 14
OBRA (Omnibus Budget
    Reconciliation Act), 19
Opportunity, as a reason to Edenize,
    96
Opportunity to care, need for, 28–29
Overmedication. *See* Drugs

*P*arakeets, 36, 128–129
    and Bob Keefe, 171–172
    and Mr. L., 45
    and Mrs. B., 57–58
    in study opposite begonia, 59
Pataki, Governor George, 169, 177
Peabody Manor, 177
Peer supervision and management,
    79
Pellets, for birds, 134
Pets. *See individual types of birds and
    animals*
Pet therapy, 111
Plagues, in nursing home, 23–25
Planters, 148–149
Plants, 143–153
    benefits of, 143–145
    epiphytes, 152–153
    growth media for, 149–150
    hanging, 145–146

life pole for, 145–146
    lighting for, 146–147
    nutrition for, 151
    obtaining, 39–40
    placement of, 145–146
    planters for, 148–149
    plastic, 39
    selecting appropriate species of,
        for nursing home, 151–153
    temperatures for, 149, 184–186
    toxic, 153
    watering, 147–149, 184–186
    when Edenizing outside the realm
        of a nursing home, 172
    windowsill, 185
Plants That Grow on Air (Kramer),
    152
Policies. *See also* Schedules; *individ-
    ual types of animals*
    Animal Diet Policy, 119
    for birds, 136
    for student volunteers, 108–110
Polypharmacy, defined, 48
Poorhouse, 13
Potting mixes, 150
Preschoolers, 42. *See also* Child care
Prescriptions. *See also* Drugs
    cost of, 50–51
    number of, 51
Principles
    of an Edenizing nursing home, 65,
        66
    of formation of Eden Alternative,
        32–33
Productivity, boosting by restructur-
    ing, 76
Psychotropic medications. *See*
    Drugs

*R*abbits, 139–140
Reason to live, as a human need, 57, 59
Recipe
    for nursing home, 9
    for soilless potting mix, 150
Reduction
    in infections, 144

in medication use, 47–53
in mortality rate, 56–57
in staff turnover, 75, 79
Regulations, and child-care centers, 102
Regulators, of nursing homes, 168–169, 176
Regulatory sanction, risk of, 167–169
Relative humidity, 144
Reorganization, of staff during Edenizing, 74–75, 76–86
Residents' rights, 69, 85, 164
Respect for the individual by leaders, 61–62
Restraints, release from, 163
Restructuring. *See* Reorganization, of staff during Edenizing
Risks, 163–169
of allergies, 165–167
as an area to address when promoting Edenizing, 96
with cats, 126
with dogs, 119–120
of illness, 164
of injury, 164–165
of legal liability, 167
of regulatory sanction, 167–169

Safety routines, 164. *See also* Objections; Risks
Savings
in decreased turnover, 75
in medication nurses, 52–53
in medications, 75
potential for national health-care system, 52
Schedules
for birds, 137
for cats, 125
for child care, 103–104
for dogs, 116
for exchange students, 108
for student volunteers, 109–110
School administration, and student volunteers, 105

Schoolchildren. *See* Children
Seed diet, 133
Self-scheduling, 73–74, 77–79
Senior management, job description of, in Edenized nursing home, 80–81. *See also* Administrators; Leadership
Sick building syndrome, 143
Siegel, Danny, 178
Social diversity, 32–33
Society finches, 131
Soil, 150
Soilless mixes, 150
Southwest Texas University, 177
Spirit, human, 62, 174
Staffing. *See also* Staff turnover
of animals, 112
and changes in duties, 52–53
Staff meetings, 67
Staff members
administrators and managers, 61–68, 70
journal entries of, 36–37
nurses and nurse aides, 71–80
as promoters of change, 94
self-scheduling by, 77–79
and team-based empowerment, 71–86
Staff turnover
of certified nurse aides, 72
of nursing middle management, 74–75, 79
reduction in, 75
States, Edenizing, 176–177
Status quo
ingredients for changing, 64–65
versus change, 63
Stein, Sara (*Noah's Garden*), 156–158
Stermer, Miriam, 177
Strangers, life among, 89–90
Stretch aerobics, 106
Summer camp, 104
Sutton's law, 9

Taking care. *See* Care versus treatment

Tanks, for fish, 141–142
Teachers, and student volunteers, 105
Team-based management. *See* Team concept
Team concept, 74–75, 76–86
  and diagrams of evolution of teams at Chase, 82–83
TEAM project (The Eden Alternative in Missouri), 176–177
Teamwork, as an operating philosophy, 63. *See also* Team concept
Temperament
  of cats, 122
  of cockatiels, 129
  of dogs, 117
  of lovebirds, 129
  of parakeets, 128–129
Texas Eden Alternative Pilot Project (TEAPP), 177
Therapy. *See* Care versus treatment
Thermostats, setting by elderly homeowners, 59
Time clock, 91–92
Total institutions, 11–13
Tranquilizers, 48–49, 52. *See also* Drugs
Transpiration, 147
Treatment. *See* Care versus treatment

Understand Your Pet: Pet Care and Humane Concerns (Fox), 129n
United States Department of Agriculture (USDA), reimbursing for meals and snacks, 102
University of Rochester, xii
Unloving Care: The Nursing Home Tragedy (Vladeck), 14n, 19
Urgency, sense of, for change, 64–65

*V*accinations
  for cats, 123
  for dogs, 117

Variety
  of dogs, 113
  human need for, 29
Vegetables, 41, 155, 156
Veterinary guidelines
  for birds, 128–129, 129n
  for cats, 123
  for dogs, 115–118
Vladeck, Bruce (*Unloving Care: The Nursing Home Tragedy*), 14n, 19
Volunteers, 106–107, 109–110

*W*heelchairs, in the garden, 160
Wilson, Roger, 198
Wolverton, Bill (article on indoor air quality), 143–144
Wood, pressure-treated, and food crops, 161

*Z*achary Test, 97
Zebra finches, 131
Ziv Tzedaka Fund, 178